As one of the world's longest established
and best-known travel brands,
Thomas Cook are the experts in travel.

For more than 135 years our
guidebooks have unlocked the secrets
of destinations around the world,
sharing with travellers a wealth of
experience and a passion for travel.

**Rely on Thomas Cook as your
travelling companion on your next trip
and benefit from our unique heritage.**

Thomas Cook **traveller** guides

CRETE
Christopher Catling

Thomas
Cook

since 1873

Written by Christopher Catling, updated by Carole French
Original photography by Philip Enticknap and Ken Paterson

Published by Thomas Cook Publishing
A division of Thomas Cook Tour Operations Limited
Company registration no. 3772199 England
The Thomas Cook Business Park, Unit 9, Coningsby Road,
Peterborough PE3 8SB, United Kingdom
Email: books@thomascook.com, Tel: + 44 (0) 1733 416477
www.thomascookpublishing.com

Produced by Cambridge Publishing Management Limited
Burr Elm Court, Main Street, Caldecote CB23 7NU
www.cambridgepm.co.uk

ISBN: 978-1-84848-364-4

© 2003, 2007, 2009 Thomas Cook Publishing
This fourth edition © 2011
Text © Thomas Cook Publishing
Maps © Thomas Cook Publishing

Series Editor: Karen Beaulah
Production/DTP: Steven Collins

Printed and bound in Spain by GraphyCems

Cover photography © Manfred Mehlig/SIME-4Corners

Contents

Introduction

Beauty, fertility and the ever-present sea – the aspects of Crete that Homer singled out for mention in the 8th century BC – are still the principal reasons why people come to Crete today. The sea gently laps the golden sands that stretch endlessly along the island's northern shores. The southern coast, by contrast, is broken into a series of smaller coves, many of them remote from any road, but perfect for creating your own private slice of paradise.

Crete's beauty and fertility are features that strike even the most botanically ignorant of visitors if they happen to arrive in spring when the fields, orchards and wayside verges turn into carpets of vividly coloured flowers. That same fertility was the source of the wealth that gave rise to the great Minoan civilisation, which dominated the Aegean from about 2600 BC until some mysterious calamity caused its destruction around 1450 BC.

Today, the Minoan palace at Knossós is the island's biggest tourist attraction, though it is just one of hundreds of sites scattered across the island – a legacy of Minoan, Roman, Venetian and Ottoman rule. In addition to this, there are some 600 churches and monasteries, many of them decorated with fragments of ancient frescoes, underlining the island's Byzantine heritage.

Exploring Crete

Many visitors come to Crete for its beaches and end up hooked on the island's culture, enjoying the adventure of tracking down a remote Minoan hilltop sanctuary, or its Christian equivalent, a tiny 12th-century church full of serene icons and wall paintings. Such explorations will take you deeper and deeper into the Cretan countryside, where the majesty of the mountain landscapes and the rhythms of the ordinary life of Crete will undoubtedly work their magic.

Nowhere is that magic more in evidence than in the simple, family-run cafés and tavernas of Crete. Choose one in a quiet fishing village and watch the sun go down as you savour the simple local food and wine while listening to the gentle wash of the waves, accompanied by the song of the cicadas. The instinctive warmth of the Cretan character adds another dimension to travel on this richly varied and rewarding island, known appropriately enough to the rest of Greece as *Megalonissos* – the Big Island.

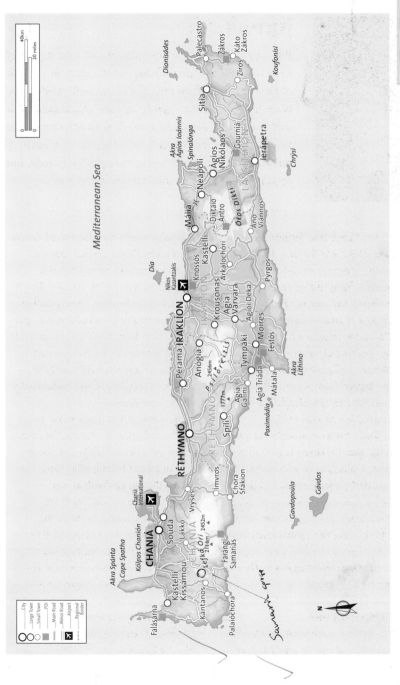

Mediterranean Sea

CHANIÁ

RÉTHYMNO

IRÁKLION

LASÍTHI

RÉTHYMNO

CHANIÁ

Falásarna

Kastélli
Kissámou

Kántanos

Palaiochóra

Soúda

Lákko

Lefká Óri 2452m
2116m

Farángi
Samariás

Vrýses

Chaniá
International

Imvros

Chóra
Sfakíon

Akra Spáda
Cape Spátha

Kólpos Chanión

Gavdopoúla

Gávdos

Spíli

Agía
Galíni

177m

Perama

Anógia

Ps. 2456m
Ídi όρεττιζ

IRÁKLION

Nikos
Kazantzakis

Dia

Tympáki

Agía Triáda

Festós

Mátala

Paximádia

Akra
Líthino

Moíres

Agioi Déka

Agía
Varvára

Krousónas

Knossós

Kastélli

Arkalochóri

Pyrgos

Ano
Viannos

Diktaío
Ántro

Óros Díkti

Mália

Neápoli

Agios Ioánnis

Spinalónga

Akra

Agios
Nikólaos

Gourniá

Ierápetra

Chrýsi

Sitía

Ziros

Zákros

Palecastro

Káto
Zákros

Koufonísi

Dionisádes

Kastélli

Samaria gorge

N

City
Large Town
Small Town
POI
Main Road
Minor Road
Regional
Border

Airport

40km

0   20 miles

The land

Crete is the largest of the hundreds of islands making up the Grecian archipelago, ranking fifth in the Mediterranean (just behind Sicily, Sardinia, Cyprus and Corsica). The island measures 250km (155 miles) from east to west, but from north to south it is only 60km (37 miles) at its widest and a mere 14km (9 miles) in places. Crete is the southernmost point of any significance in Europe.

Mountains and caves

Distances on Crete are greatly magnified by the mountain ranges that run like a spine down the centre of the island, acting as a barrier to north–south travel. The southern part of the island has always been more remote and less populated than the north, though this is changing as the little fishing villages of the south are discovered by tourists looking for a quiet base.

Crete's mountains are a continuation of the same chain that sweeps down from the Peloponnese, surfacing again on the islands of Karpathos and Rhodes. They are composed principally of limestone that has been eroded into the spectacular gorges and caves.

It was in one of these caves (the Díktaean – *see pp80–81*) that Zeus, destined to rule over the ancient gods, was born. The story of Zeus is perhaps a mythic throwback to the origin of human life on Crete, since many of the island's caves have revealed extensive evidence of Neolithic occupation.

Vegetation

The name of the Ídaean Cave (*see pp132–3*) preserves another memory of the old Crete: *idha* means forest in Doric Greek, and Herodotus, the 5th-century BC Greek historian, refers to Crete as being covered in trees. The island was still well wooded when the Venetians arrived in the 13th century, but their voracious appetite for ship-building timber, combined with an extensive building programme, began the steady erosion of the indigenous vegetation. Today, only small patches of the original forest survive, consisting of cypress, Calabrian pine and evergreen holm oak, with plane, sweet chestnut and introduced eucalyptus in the river valleys. Out of the 2,000 species that can be found on Crete, 160 of them are endemic to the island. Taking their cue from the island's ancient forest mix, road builders have planted many new trees to create attractive groves along the verges of the national highway.

The Phrygana

Those areas of Crete that are not under cultivation are covered in a scrub called the *phrygana*, the Cretan equivalent to the *maquis* that covers many parts of the Mediterranean. This fragrant mass of wild plants includes many shrubs that are resistant to the island's sheep and goats. Prickly kermes oak and bitter-tasting euphorbias cover the hillsides in dense billowing mounds of green, with other plants sheltering in and among them to take advantage of their protection. These include fragrant herbs such as mint, oregano, sage and thyme, shrubs such as phlomis and cistus, and the wonderful range of wild flowers, bulbs and orchids for which Crete is renowned.

Wildlife

The *phrygana* was once home to the splendidly horned Cretan ibex, or *krí-krí*, depicted in Minoan art (see, for example, the Peak Sanctuary Rhyton in Iraklíon's Archaeological Museum, *p31*). Walkers on Crete frequently claim to have seen this shy and elusive animal, but they are now virtually extinct on Crete, surviving only in special offshore nature reserves, such as Ayíi Pántes (*see p86*). You are quite likely to spot harmless basking snakes, geckos and wall lizards, and even the occasional chameleon, for though this reptile is a master of camouflage, it gives its presence away by running noisily through the undergrowth. Polecats are common, but more likely to be seen as a roadside accident victim than as a live animal, while the sky is rarely empty of wheeling eagles and vultures searching for young rabbits and other prey.

Typical Cretan scrub, full of tough but fragrant flowering plants

History

6000 BC	Earliest known villages on Crete; Neolithic pottery and figurines.	**1380 BC**	Eruption of the volcano on Théra (Santoríni) to which archaeologists of the 19th century attributed the end of Minoan civilisation.
Around 3000 BC	Migrants to Crete establish the first Minoan settlements. The beginning of the pre-Palatial period.	**1050 BC**	Dorian Greeks arrive in Crete.
2200 BC	First peak sanctuaries and use of hieroglyphic script.	**650 BC**	Extensive trade with Egypt is reflected in the Egyptian influence on Dorian-period art.
2000 BC	Beginning of the Old Palace period; trade links with Egypt and the Aegean islands.	**450 BC**	The Law Code of Gortýs is carved in stone.
1700 BC	Beginning of the New Palace period.	**69–67 BC**	Quintus Metellus invades Crete and ruthlessly destroys many towns and villages. The city of Gortýs becomes the new capital of Roman Crete.
1650 BC	First use of Linear A script.		
1550 BC	Artistic peak of Minoan pottery and fresco.	**AD 50**	St Paul visits Crete and sends St Titus to convert the island's inhabitants to Christianity.
1450 BC	Beginning of the post-Palatial period during which Minoan culture lingered in isolated areas for another 400 years.	**395**	Crete comes under eastern Byzantine control and the island's first churches are established.
1400 BC	Mycenaeans (also known as Achaians) take over the island. Creation of the Linear B script.	**824**	Crete is invaded by the Arabs who use Al-Khandak

(Iraklíon) as a base for piratical attacks.

961   The Byzantine general, Nikiforos Fokas, liberates Crete from the Arabs. Byzantine culture begins.

1204   Crete is given to one of the Fourth Crusade leaders, Boniface of Montferrat, as his share in the spoils of the war, and he sells the island to Venice.

1263   As a punishment for revolts against Venetian rule, the villages of the Lassíthi Plateau are forcibly depopulated and nobody is allowed to farm the area for 200 years.

1453   Constantinople falls to the Ottomans and Byzantine scholars escape to Crete.

1645   The Ottomans begin their long assault on Crete, taking Chaniá and Réthymno.

1669   Crete finally falls to the Ottomans.

1841   First revolt against the Ottomans in Crete in support of Enôsis – union with Greece.

1898   Britain, France, Russia and Italy occupy Crete and force the Ottoman Turks to recognise Crete's right to autonomy.

1900   Arthur Evans begins excavating Knossós.

1913   The Ottomans are forced to surrender sovereignty over Crete.

1941   Cretan resistance against occupying German forces brings appalling reprisals.

1945   The Liberation of Crete.

1983   Mass tourism arrives on Crete, with visitor numbers exceeding 1 million (double the Cretan population) for the first time.

2004/5   Tourism dips during the Athens 2004 Olympic Games but recovers the following year.

2012   Expected reopening of the Iraklíon Archaeological Museum.

2014   New international airport due to open near Kastélli.

The Minoans

Crete is the birthplace of Europe's oldest civilisation, though no one suspected this until the late 19th century when foreigners were first given permission to conduct limited excavations on the island. Early archaeologists were astounded to discover, not the classical Greek sites they had been expecting, but the accomplished art and architecture of a far older civilisation, comparable in achievement with the other great ancient civilisations of China, Egypt and Mesopotamia.

Priests, kings and matriarchs

Arthur Evans (*see pp56–7*) called this culture Minoan after Minos, the legendary king of Crete. Scholars now believe that Minos was not the name of one man, but the title given to all rulers, like the Egyptian term Pharaoh. Minoan rulers were also priests, and their palaces (at Knossós, Mália, Festós and Zákros) were centres for elaborate rituals, in which acrobatic bull-leaping had an important part to play.

This was just one feature of their many-faceted religion: women clearly played an important role, and two of the commonest finds from Minoan temples and peak sanctuaries are clay figures of the bare-breasted Snake Goddess and figures of male devotees with erect penises or large codpieces. Olive trees, which frequently figure in Minoan frescoes and on seals, were also worshipped. All this lends weight to the theory that Minoan religion was rooted in the cycle of the seasons, and that the palaces were centres of annual fertility rituals designed to ensure the success of crops.

Old and new palaces

In Minoan chronology, the Old Palace period, from 2000 to 1700 BC, saw the development of massive palaces built around a courtyard, surrounded by clusters of smaller houses and workshops. In 1700 BC an earthquake brought these elaborate edifices tumbling down. During the New Palace period, from 1700 to 1400 BC, the palaces were rebuilt, more elaborate than before, with delicate frescoes and fine furnishings.

Resources and revolution

Minoan society was highly organised, and the power of the priests was based on their control of precious commodities, such as olive oil and wine. Oil was kept in vast quantities in huge jars (*píthoi*) in palace storerooms. The presence of so much flammable oil contributed greatly to the final destruction of the Minoan civilisation in 1450 BC when fire swept through the palaces.

Evidence of the fires is plain to see at the Minoan palace sites, but their precise cause is shrouded in speculation and mystery. Evans confidently blamed the eruption of Théra (Santoríni), but that took place in around 1380 BC. Other historians have put forward the theory that the island was invaded and sacked, perhaps by the Mycenaeans who later came to control Crete, but there is no archaeological evidence to support this.

Post-Palatial period

In the post-Palatial period, from 1400 to 1100 BC, the Mycenaeans took advantage of the disaster that befell Crete and moved in, briefly occupying the palace at Knossós and using it as the administrative centre of the island until 1200 BC when they finally abandoned it. Some peak sanctuaries continued in use, and there are echoes of the Minoan golden age in the Mycenaean-influenced sculpture and pottery of this era.

Some Cretans clung on to the old ways for generations; they are mentioned in Homer's *Odyssey* (written around 700 BC) where, when writing about the Minoans and Mycenaeans who live on Crete, he mentions the 'Etocretans (i.e. the true, or genuine, Cretans), proud of their native stock'. Right up until the 3rd century BC, they maintained their own separate language and script, dubbed Linear B, which is seen on inscriptions that have been found at Praisós and Dréros. It intrigued archaeologists for a long time until finally deciphered by Professor John Chadwick and architect Mark Ventris in 1952.

The west façade and grand staircase of the palace at Festós

Politics

Cretans are a fiercely proud and independent-minded people who, in the words of a popular phrase, see themselves as 'Cretans first, Greeks second'. They are also fond of naming their children Eleftherias (Freedom) and of quoting the patriotic slogan, 'Freedom or Death', that anti-Turkish rebels adopted as their battle cry in the 19th century. In reality, Cretans have experienced little in the way of true political freedom over the last 3,500 years.

A history of oppression

Since the collapse of the Minoan civilisation, the island has been ruled by one foreign power after another – Mycenaeans, Dorian Greeks, Egyptians, Romans, Arabs, Byzantines, Venetians and Ottomans.

The 20th century brought long-awaited unification with the rest of Greece, and the Cretan statesman, Eleftherias Venizélos, served as prime minister of Greece on numerous occasions, playing a central role in national politics and foreign affairs between 1896 and 1935.

Following World War II and invasion by Germany (*see pp104–5*), Crete came under the Greek Colonels' dictatorship from 1967 until 1974. That year, following a popular referendum, Greece abolished the monarchy and, along with Crete, become a parliamentary democracy, headed by a president.

National government

Even now, Crete has little political autonomy, for Greece has a strongly centralised government, with a parliament in Athens. Crete sends elected representatives, called deputies, to the parliament, and one Cretan politician, Kostas Mitsotakis, rose to lead the right-of-centre ND (Néa Dhimokratía, or New Democracy) party which narrowly won the 1990 election. The other dominant political force is PASOK (The Panhellenic Socialist

Plateía Eleftherías (Freedom Square), Iraklíon

The PASOK party's sunrise symbol

Movement). Its founder, Andreas Papandreou, was succeeded in 1996 by Costas Simitis, who modernised the party and was successful in two general elections. Despite his record, however, PASOK was voted out in 2004 and, in 2007, suffered their worst defeat in 30 years as the ND party was re-elected.

Local government

Crete has no independent regional government, and is ruled instead by governors appointed by the ruling party in Athens. There is one governor for each of the island's four provinces (*nomoi*), namely Chaniá, Réthymno, Iraklíon and Lassíthiou. In the past, Cretan governors and political leaders modelled themselves on the clan leaders of old, whose proud portraits look down from the walls of the history museums in Chaniá and Iraklíon. Refusing to be 'yes men', they have frequently defied the national party line

in the greater interests of Crete. That is changing, however, and the availability of new development funds from the European Union (EU) means that their energies are focused on securing the maximum benefit for the island.

Among current initiatives is the EU Cohesion Policy 2007–2013. This project, which has provided multi-euro investment for modernising Crete's infrastructure, is designed to encourage private investment in the island, enhance environmental management, and promote the use of information and communication technology.

Crete as a military base

Though the presence of large numbers of NATO military personnel and weaponry is hotly debated, Cretans are only too well aware that they stand between the Islamic world and the West, and are therefore a potential target in the event of aggression.

Culture

On Crete two separate cultures coexist side by side: the Crete of the 21st century and the rural, pre-industrial Crete, which has not changed much, in any significant way, since Minoan times.

Country life

In the heart of rural Crete there are still many people, mainly elderly now, who live a very meagre, self-sufficient life. Their food comes from what they grow, or gather wild. Though every village now has electricity, homes are simple and cooking is still done over a wood fire. They rarely travel far beyond their home village, and when they do, they go by donkey, which also serves as an all-purpose pack animal.

These people are the survivors of the old Cretan way of life. Their children have left this (and them) behind, seeking paid work and an air-conditioned apartment in one of Crete's burgeoning towns, working in IT, web design or tourism, or doing a PhD in ancient Greek. The remaining rural Cretans claim to have an egalitarian society, without class distinctions or rancour, and the warm-heartedness of their easy-going hospitality appears to bear this out. They attribute their way of life to centuries of subjugation to foreign rulers, especially the harsh and oppressive Ottomans. Taxed into abject poverty and denied education or legal rights, they developed their own unwritten codes of honour, mutual respect and cooperation that have survived to this day.

The *kafenion*

Within this society, the *kafenion*, or café, also serves the purpose of local parliament. The typical village *kafenion* is as plain as can be: no posters adorn the walls and there are no price lists or tempting bottles of exotic drinks on display. Local wine, coffee and water are the principal drinks on offer: customers can linger for hours over one small drink and nobody will object. On the contrary, it would be thought odd not to linger, since the *kafenion* is the local club, a place where men can gather to spend the whole evening in talk or play a game of backgammon. Cafés are traditionally male-dominated establishments.

The *voltá*

Women have their equivalent in the *voltá*, the evening stroll, a habit influenced by the Italian *passeggiata*, introduced by the Venetians. The *voltá* takes place at that delightful hour of the day when darkness begins to fall and work is done. As the sun sets and the swifts flit above the tree tops, women take off their aprons, brush their hair and step out of doors. Taking their children, they stroll arm in arm to greet old friends, to gossip or, if they are still young and single, to flirt.

Country versus town

The *voltá* and the *kafeníon* are the two traditions that still link the old Crete with the new. The evening stroll in Réthymno is especially vibrant, and the large number of students in both Chaniá and Réthymno help to ensure that the cafés used by local people are always full – especially late at night, long after hard-working rural Cretans have gone to bed. Country rarely meets town except for village festivities, weddings, baptisms and funerals, or on the one day a week (often a Saturday) when rural Cretans descend on their nearest big town to set up street stalls selling everything from honey, olives and dried herbs, to leather boots and hand-knitted sweaters. Arriving the night before market day, many give up the attempt to snatch some sleep in the back of their van or pick-up truck, drifting to the local cafés where the music and dancing go on until the first light of dawn.

Farming the old way

Tapestry depicting a well-dressed Cretan couple

Customs and etiquette

Cretan people are very friendly, if a little shy, on meeting strangers. A wave or a nod as you pass someone while out walking usually elicits a broad smile. If you say hello in Greek (*yásou*), all the better. Don't be surprised to be offered a piece of fruit off somebody's orange tree or a glass of *raki* on the house in a restaurant – or even a little extra dish you did not order. Such spontaneous generosity is still quite common, especially in the parts of Crete not tainted by mass tourism. Cretans love to practise their English, so take the time to chat – about the weather, children, your job – all are subjects with endless potential.

Costume

Cretan costume is still worn with pride by some country Cretans, especially by the older men who gather to pass the day playing backgammon in the *kafeníon*. Prior to the Ottoman occupation of Crete, dress consisted of a simple belted tunic for both men and women. Examples can be seen in many church frescoes throughout the island. Typically, the donor of the fresco (and his wife) is depicted beside the door of the church, and these portraits show that costume changed little in the period from the 11th to the 16th century (copies of these are displayed in Iraklíon's Historical Museum – *see pp33–4*).

Turkish fashions

The Ottomans introduced baggy breeches (called *vraka*), which Cretans adopted in a major break with their past. Ironically, it was the anti-Ottoman rebels who were keenest on this new fashion (today, Cretan men are more likely to wear ordinary riding breeches). Waistcoats are worn over a simple shirt by men and women alike, usually embroidered with colourful motifs that differ from region to region. Women also wear skirts of brightly coloured stripes, protected by a simple apron. Men adopted the black crochet-work cap with its distinctive fringe as a symbol of mourning for their island under Ottoman occupation, though the cap continues to be worn to this day.

Daggers and boots

On special occasions (such as weddings and feast days), men still wear a big silk sash around their waist, into which they tuck a whole collection of heirlooms – perhaps a tobacco horn, perhaps a silver dagger or a pistol (often an antique 18th-century weapon, last used in World War II). Smart and highly polished riding boots complete the picture, along with a moustache. Fine examples of historic costume are displayed in the Historical Museums at Iráklion (*see pp33–4*), Chaniá (*see p95*), and at the Museum of Cretan Ethnology in Vóroi (*see p64*).

The Cretan shepherd

Drive along any rural road in Crete and it will not be long before you encounter a flock of sheep or goats with an attendant shepherd, probably seated nearby beneath the shade of an olive tree. Stop on any rural road and you will hear the musical clamour of bells. Traditionally, long bells are hung round the necks of goats and wide ones round sheep, with seven different sizes and notes so that the shepherd can identify each individual in his flock. The shepherd who spends his lifetime looking after these hardy foragers will probably be dressed in a fine pair of knee boots, baggy Cretan pantaloons, and lace headcap if he is over 40 years of age, and nearby will be a donkey carrying a wooden pack saddle and panniers. Times are changing, however, and younger shepherds are more likely to be dressed in jeans and trainers and driving a pick-up truck. Regardless of age, all shepherds carry the ubiquitous crook, whose shape varies from region to region.

Shepherding is a hard and lonely life, and although both lamb and *feta* cheese are staples of the Cretan diet, it is rare to find a wealthy farmer – one reason why fewer and fewer young people take up shepherding, aspiring instead to a more comfortable office job.

The lonely figure of a shepherd searching for green pastures

Festivals

Easter is the big festival on Crete and many people come to the island just for this seven-day period of religious and secular spectacle. Bear in mind, though, that the dates of Easter and most other religious festivals vary from year to year, and very rarely coincide with those of the calendar of the Western Church.

Easter rites

Good Friday (Epitafiós) is marked by solemn processions in which a shrouded bier, representing the dead Christ, is carried around the village to the accompaniment of prayers and mournful song. At midnight the following day, Easter Saturday, all lights are extinguished and the priest produces the first flame of the new Christian year, symbolising resurrection and renewal. Holy Light, as this is called, is brought from Jerusalem where the first holy candle is lit.

A traditional Easter breakfast of red-dyed eggs

Members of the congregation light their candles from this flame to the chant of *Khristós anésti* (Christ is Risen). This marks the end of the service, when church bells peal, firecrackers explode and, in some districts, bonfires are lit on which a dummy, representing Judas, the disciple who betrayed Christ, is burnt. Easter Sunday is then spent in feasting, traditionally on spit-roasted lamb.

Saints' days

Lamb features again on the Feast of Ágios Giórgios (St George, celebrated on 23 April, or, if Orthodox Easter happens to be very late in the month, on the Monday and Tuesday after Easter Sunday). St George is very popular on Crete because, among his many other responsibilities, he is the patron of shepherds. Sheep and goat farmers take their flocks to church to be blessed, and one of their number is sacrificed to provide the traditional St George's Day dish of charcoal-grilled, herb-and-rice-stuffed lamb.

Every Cretan village also celebrates its own saint's day with a church service followed by singing, dancing, drinking and feasting. Visitors are warmly welcomed, so ask at the tourist office for details of any village name days coming up in the vicinity at the time of your visit. One that is certain to be celebrated all over the island, given that many churches are dedicated to the Panagia (the Virgin Mary), is 15 August, the Feast of the Assumption.

Wine and food

Among the most appealing festivals for atmosphere are those held in different parts of the island from early August to the end of October, an excuse for finishing off last year's wine and sampling this year's *raki*. More of an acquired taste is *Kholidovradia* (The Night of the Snails), celebrated by the mollusc-loving inhabitants of Vámos in April. Autumn brings the chestnut harvest in Élos, and with it an excuse to eat chestnut-flavoured sweets of all kinds, washed down with yet more *raki*, on the first Sunday after 20 October.

Arts festivals

Throughout the main holiday month of August, major towns mount one- or two-week arts festivals; a feast of dancing, parades, music, theatre, and exhibitions of paintings and crafts.

Traditional dance plays an important role in Cretan life

Impressions

The idea of touring Crete by car and stopping somewhere different every night has become very popular. The increase in direct and low-cost scheduled flights to Crete, as well as more charter flight deals, means tourists have plenty of travel options, whether they choose a package or organise their trip independently. Island wandering is recommended, especially during the shoulder period when hotels have rooms to spare and temperatures are ideal for walking.

Crete's tourist season lasts from April to October. However, the island is currently embarking on a winter pilot programme to encourage year-round tourism, and more upmarket resorts and boutique hotels have been built.

East or west, north or south?

An alternative to going wherever you please is to choose one hotel or villa that is centrally located for the area you want to explore. This means basing yourself in the north of the island where the national highway provides a relatively swift route from east to west. Crete is not so large that you can't see much of it in a fortnight, although many travellers spend up to two weeks exploring the eastern or the western half of the island, so choose your base accordingly.

The east and centre of Crete is best for those who want to see the main archaeological sites. To explore this region, you could do worse than choose a base on the coastal strip between Iraklíon and Ágios Nikólaos. Here you will be within easy reach of the palaces at Knossós, Mália, Festós and Zákros, and within easy driving distance of the Lassíthiou Plateau and Díktaean Cave (Dhiktaio Andro). Be warned, though, that the north is the most developed part of Crete, so you have to choose your base carefully, paying more, perhaps, for a villa in a village rather than ending up in a cheap but anonymous apartment in one of the tourist ghettos, such as Mália and Chersonísou.

Hiking and flowers

The further west you go on Crete, the quieter it gets, although there is another flurry of tourist development around Chaniá. Western Crete is generally greener, more mountainous and less intensively farmed than the plains that make up so much of eastern Crete. Nature lovers will find that the west is richer, botanically, and for historically inclined visitors, there is a greater concentration of Byzantine churches to explore. Above all, this is the region for long and spectacular walks through the Samaria and Ímvros gorges (Farángi Samariás and Farángi Ímvros), or out along the finger-like peninsulas of the northern coast.

Beach holidays

If you just want to drop out and do nothing more energetic than strolling to the beach each day, there are scores of Mediterranean hideaways in the less developed extremities of the island, from Vái, in the extreme east, to the Elafonísi islands in the extreme west. Most are on the south side of the island, with characterful fishing villages such as Palaióchora and Chóra Sfakíon, known for their unspoilt Cretan character, good shops, food and nightlife. Accommodation availability in these villages is limited, so book early in high season; the rest of the year you may be able to turn up in a town and find rooms to rent there and then.

Getting around

If you know you want to do a lot of driving on Crete, it is cheaper to pre-book a hire car online or as part of a package. However, if you decide to wait until you arrive in Crete, you will find scores of car rental agents at the airport and on the main street of every town.

It is vital to check the state of the tyres (including the spare) before

Cruising to Eloúnta is a good way to see the picturesque coast

Rural churches may be difficult to reach but are usually open all the time

setting out on any journey, and be sure that you know how to use the jack – potholes and sharp stones make punctures on Crete's rural roads common. Motorbikes and scooters are also readily available for hire, but are not suitable for long journeys. Despite the fact that many Cretans break the law, wearing a helmet is compulsory – ensure that the hire company gives you one that fits you comfortably and is not damaged.

Museums and archaeological sites

Cretans are early risers, making the most of the coolest part of the day and taking a long siesta during the afternoon. Opening times reflect this, with many museums and sites open for the morning and early afternoon only (typically 8.30am–3pm).

Photography is not always permitted in museums. However, professional photographers may apply for special permission from the Ministry of Culture.

Officially, it is forbidden to climb on the walls at archaeological sites, but this rule is widely ignored. You will also find that sites are, quite literally, littered with pieces of ancient pottery. Do not give in to temptation – picking them up is also against the law, as is any kind of unlicensed digging.

Monasteries and churches

Monasteries are generally open to visitors from 8am to 1pm or 2pm, though some reopen at 3pm or 5pm until 7pm. All insist on modest dress (shorts, sleeveless shirts and beachwear are forbidden) so it is sensible to carry a change of clothes if you go visiting a monastery. Women are also not allowed to enter some.

The opening arrangements for churches vary considerably. Some are open all the time, but many are kept locked. It is common practice to begin the hunt for the key (*kleidí*) at the nearest *kafeníon* (café), but it is not good manners to do so during the 1–4pm siesta hours.

Often the key is held by the local priest (*pappás*) who may accompany you to the church and provide an enthusiastic commentary, in broken English, on the principal frescoes and icons. If so, you will be expected to give the priest a small donation towards church funds. Remember, too, that women are not supposed to enter the sanctuary (the area behind the iconostasis, or screen) unless invited.

Impressions

A typical Byzantine church at Samonás

Eastern Crete

Eastern Crete is made up of the two provinces (nomoi) of Iraklíon and Lassíthiou. This is the most heavily populated part of the island, with 303,000 people living in Iraklíon province (150,000 of them in Iraklíon city alone) and 78,000 in Lassíthiou (19,000 in the capital, Ágios Nikólaos). Together, these two provinces account for over 70 per cent of the total Cretan population of 630,000.

The resort coast

The city of Iraklíon is the main gateway to the island, with a ferry port and international airport. Around 70 per cent of the 2 million tourists who come to Crete every year stay in one of the resorts strung out along the 70km (43-mile) coastal strip east of Iraklíon, especially the resort towns of Chersonísou, Mália, Eloúnta and Ágios Nikólaos. Staying in any of these places you will not lack for shops, nightlife or the company of fellow visitors, but you will experience very little of the true Crete.

Beaches

The coastal strip east of Iraklíon is one long series of resorts offering shops, fast-food outlets, and beach loungers for hire. To escape the crowds, head for the far east of the island, or the less developed beaches on the south coast. Remoteness does not guarantee isolation, however: the so-called Palm Beach at Vaí and the beach at Préveli are among the most crowded on the island at peak season. Bathing nude is strictly forbidden.

The south coast

This being Crete, the opportunity to escape from the crowds is never very far away, and true solitude can be experienced on the far eastern and southern coasts, much of which is accessible only by small, winding roads. Here, adventurous travellers can track down hermits' caves and monasteries clinging to the cliffs.

How long this will continue to be true remains to be seen. Bulldozers are always opening up new roads and concrete villas are spreading rapidly around any tiny village with access to a sandy beach. Tourism is increasing along the southern coast, and in the fairly unspoilt southeastern corner of the island with increased use of the airport at Sitía. At present, though, development is still fairly slow, and tourism steady rather than booming.

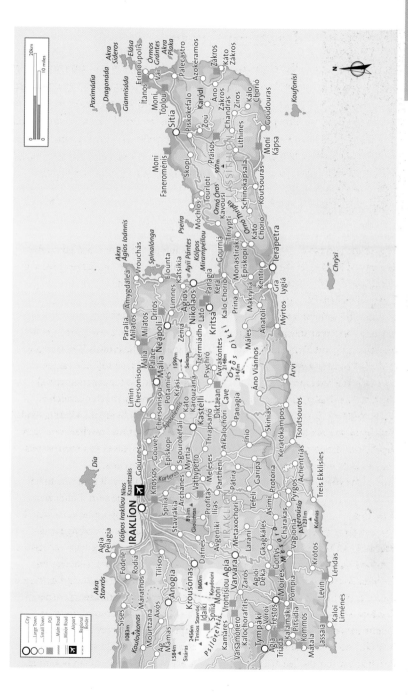

IRAKLÍON PROVINCE

It was here that the Minoan civilisation first arose and where the most spectacular archaeological sites are to be found. Three of the four major Minoan palaces, which formed the focal point for Minoan art and industry, are located here (at Knossós, Mália and Festós), along with smaller palace complexes at Agía Triáda and Archánes. Festós and Agía Triáda enjoy the most spectacular locations on the fertile agricultural plain on Messará.

Iraklíon

Iraklíon, capital of Crete, is the fifth-largest city in Greece. The air raids of 1941 reduced the city to rubble so that it lacks the old-world charm of Réthymno or Chaniá. Though no great beauty, Iraklíon can at least claim to be prosperous, with the highest per capita income of any city in Greece, derived from a combination of shipping, banking and tourism. The city's star attraction is the Archaeological Museum (*see pp29–32*), full of Minoan treasures, many excavated at Knossós (*see pp50–55*) just 5km (3 miles) to the south.

The harbour

Iraklíon's historic harbour bustles with luxury yachts and fishing boats unloading their catch beneath the walls of the bulky Venetian Fortress, Koúles. The first fort was built here in 1303 but was later destroyed by an earthquake. Rebuilt between 1523 and 1540, the fort was to play a key role in the Great Siege of 1647–69. At the end of this 22-year siege, among the longest in history, the Venetians finally gave up one of their most precious possessions, surrendering Iraklíon (and Crete) to the Ottomans, but only after heroic resistance, in which 30,000 Venetians and 118,000 Ottomans met their deaths. The new Turkish rulers of Iraklíon changed little, and even the Lion of St Mark, symbol of Venice, still stands guard over the entrance to the fort.

Another legacy of Venetian rule is the 16th-century *Arsenali* (Arsenal) where ships of the Venetian naval fleet were once built, repaired and fitted out for battle. A busy road has since cut these huge vaulted buildings off from the harbour, but they remain an impressive tribute to Venetian marine engineering. They are currently being renovated. *Venetian fort open: Apr–Oct, daily 8.30am–3pm. Closed: Sun in winter. Admission charge.*

IRAKLÍON'S NAME

The bustling capital of Crete started out as a Minoan harbour, named Heraklion (city of Herakles, that is, Hercules) by the Dorian Greeks. In 824, under Saracen rule, it became Rabdh el Khanadak (Castle of the Ditch), was corrupted to Khandakas and, later, under Venetian rule, to Candia. This was the name under which the city, and the whole island, was known until the end of Turkish rule in 1898, when the Dorian Greek name was revived, as Iraklíon in modern Greek spelling.

Iraklíon town plan (*see pp38–9 for walk route*)

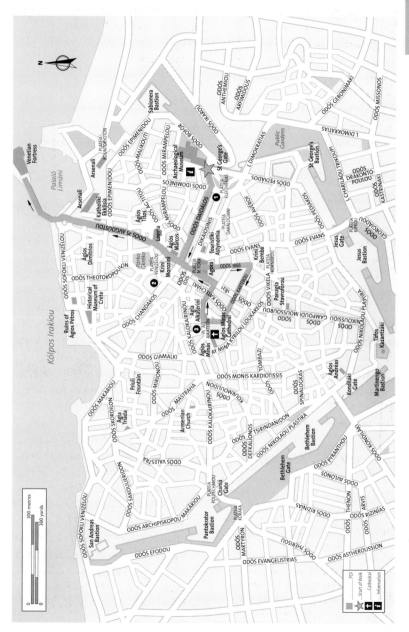

The ramparts and tomb of Kazantzákis

Contemporary with the fortress and the Arsenal are the walls that enclose Iraklíon for a total length of 3km (2 miles). It is possible to walk the complete circuit for views of city gardens and rooftops, but in order to gain a sense of the massive proportions of the walls, it is best to visit Porta Kenoúria, the gate on Odós Evans in the south of the city. Built in

Yachts and fishing boats moor beneath the protective walls of Iraklíon's Venetian Fortress

1538 by the great Italian architect Michele Sanmicheli, the walls stand 18m (59ft) tall and over 40m (131ft) thick. On the Martinengo Bastion, five minutes' walk to the southwest, is the simple grave of the Cretan novelist Níkos Kazantzákis (*see pp61 & 64*). He was buried here at his own request, and the inscription on his tomb says much about the Cretan attitude to life and mortality: 'I hope for nothing, I fear nothing, I am free.'

Archaeological Museum

This is rated one of the top museums in Greece because of the quality of the objects on display. However, the museum is undergoing massive reconstruction, so, until the new space opens, which is not expected until at least 2012, a temporary annexe will house the most important pieces. The sheer number of visitors can be a problem, so allow longer than you would expect to tour the museum, or come during lunch hour when there are far fewer tour groups.

Room I This room is devoted to the Neolithic and pre-Palatial phase of Cretan history (6000–2000 BC). Here we see the first depictions of bulls and acrobats; of the female fertility deity with exaggerated hips, breasts and buttocks; of the symbolic double-bladed axe; and of the *moclos* – the sacred double horn emblem. These motifs recur again and again, honed and refined over 3,000 years of production.

Among the assorted exhibits, the highlights are the pottery rattle (between Cases 4 and 5), with a tracing alongside of the scene from the Harvester Vase (*see* Room VII *p31*), showing such a rattle in use; and the wonderfully naturalistic pot lid in Case 7 with a handle shaped like a dog.

Rooms II and III These two rooms are devoted to the Old Palace period (2000–1700 BC). A delightful insight into the sophistication of architecture at the time is given by the so-called Town Mosaic (Case 25), consisting of a number of pottery squares painted with representations of Minoan houses.

There are numerous clay figurines from peak sanctuaries, pointing to their heads or stomachs, perhaps indicating bits of their bodies that they want curing. Women wear bell-shaped skirts and place their hands under their breasts, pushing them up in a gesture of offering, while men have erect penises or large codpieces.

Room III contains masterpieces of Minoan pottery, such as the vase with the daisy motif (Case 36) and the lifelike clay pig in the last case on the right. Here too is the famous circular clay disc from Festós (Case 41), bearing a stamped inscription that has so far defeated all attempts at interpretation.

Room IV This is the first of six rooms devoted to the New Palace period (1700–1450 BC), with outstanding works from the palace at Knossós. One is a gaming board made of ivory and precious stone (Case 57). In Case 49 is a lovely vase covered in an all-over pattern of bamboo leaves. Case 51 contains the famous Bull's Head Rhyton, a gentle-looking beast carved out of steatite, with gilded wooden horns, rock-crystal eyes and inlaid shell nostrils. Sacred libations – perhaps of bull's blood or wine – were poured from a hole behind the horns.

Case 56 contains a delicate ivory figure of an acrobat flying through the air in mid-manoeuvre, probably having launched himself from the horns of a bull. Case 52 is full of stone vases covered in intricate designs – see the one entitled 'The Entrapped Octopus', for example.

Headless statue outside the Iraklion Archaeological Museum

Case 50 brings us face to face with the Snake Goddess, a frightening figure with bulging eyes that seek to entrance the onlooker – or is it the goddess herself that is in a trance? Next to her is a similar figure with snakes entwining her hair, dress and belt.

Room V This room contains material excavated from parts of Knossós away from the main palace, including the workshops and houses lining the Royal Road. An idea of what these houses may have looked like is indicated by the clay model in Case 70a. Pictures on the walls of this room show reconstructions of various parts of Knossós drawn by Piet de Jong, the draughtsman who worked with Sir Arthur Evans during the excavation of the site.

Room VI Here the most rewarding exhibits are in the central cases, where gold and ivory jewellery is displayed, including necklace ornaments and rings shaped like shells, bulls' heads, lions and ducks.

Room VII This contains the finest example of Minoan jewellery ever found, an exquisite pendant of gold depicting two bees, joined at the mouth and tail, leaving a drop of honey on a honeycomb held between their legs (Case 101). Equally enthralling are three stone vases. The subject of the Chieftain Cup (Case 95) is still being debated: does it show a hunting party, or a Minoan chieftain being presented

Iraklíon's Archaeological Museum is a storehouse of ancient sculpture and arts

with hides as some form of tax or tribute? The Boxer Rhyton (Case 96) shows the now-familiar sport of bull-leaping, as well as scenes of boxing and wrestling. The marvellous Harvester Vase (Case 94) shows a procession of youths carrying rods and pitchforks, accompanied by singers and musicians, taking part in some kind of harvest festival.

Room VIII The finest of all the Minoan libation vases is the Peak Sanctuary Rhyton (Case 111). Not only is the carving wonderfully naturalistic, with wild tulips blossoming from the craggy heights, Cretan wild goats with magnificent horns resting on the mountain ridges, and crows using the sacred bull's horn symbol on the temple roof as a perch, it also provides a detailed view of the appearance of a Minoan peak

sanctuary of the type otherwise known only from excavated ruins.

Also in this room are numerous fine examples of pottery shaped like shells and decorated with marine symbols, and the famous libation vase of black crystal – the finest piece to be found in the Zákros Palace.

Room IX The marine motifs continue with an especially enjoyable octopus flask to be found in Case 120.

Rooms X to XIII Exhibits dating to the post-Minoan era (1400–500 BC) show new developments, and the introduction of Egyptian influences to Minoan art. Though the objects are more primitive, and the decoration more debased, there are some unusual figures, including the Poppy Goddess (Room X, Case 133) and the woman on a swing (Room X, Case 143). The displays on the ground floor end with a roomful of clay sarcophagi, shaped like bathtubs.

Rooms XIV to XVI Much of the first floor of the museum is devoted to Minoan frescoes, forming the highlight of the collection. The archaeologists who reconstructed these works, often from a tiny handful of fragments, have been accused of using their imaginations too freely, but it is difficult not to be moved by the great vibrancy and naturalism displayed by the Partridge Frieze, or the Leaping Dolphins.

Problems of interpretation are well illustrated by the display in Room XVI where a fresco, previously thought to depict a boy picking flowers (entitled the 'Saffron Gatherer'), has now been reassembled to create a bigger picture called the 'Blue Monkey', set in a landscape of rocks and crocuses.

Classical Greek heads and sculptured stone bear testimony to the artisan's skill

Completely original is the wonderful stone sarcophagus in the centre of Room XIV, its painted decoration of aquamarine blue and ox-blood red still remarkably fresh. The long sides depict a funeral procession in great detail, showing a horse-drawn chariot, the sacrifice of a young bull and various musical instruments.

Rooms XVII to XX The last part of the museum is devoted to Greek and Roman antiquities, which seem almost lifeless compared with the exuberance of the preceding frescoes. An occasional exhibit stands out, such as the life-size statue of a boy in bronze (Room XVIII), found at Ierápetra and dating from the 1st century BC.

Plateía Eleftherias. Tel: (2810) 226092. The old museum building is closed for major renovation until at least 2012. There is a superb highlights exhibition in the adjoining modern building. Open: summer Tue–Sun 8am–8pm, Mon 1.30–8pm; winter Tue–Sun 8.30am–3pm. Telephone for latest information.

El Greco's *View of Mount Sinai and the Monastery* in the Historical Museum of Crete

The Historical Museum of Crete

The Historical Museum takes up where the Archaeological Museum (*see p29*) leaves off, and follows Crete's chequered history into the 20th century.

Basement This area displays sculptures and architectural fragments dating back to the Venetian occupation of the island. Doorways and windows, angels, saints, coats of arms, and tombstones bearing Turkish, Armenian and Jewish inscriptions, indicate the cosmopolitan nature of the island's port.

Ground floor The excellent new AG Kalokairinos room covers the Christian period, with emphasis on Venetian rule and the Cretan War (1645–69). Exhibits include a large, detailed model of Candia (as Iraklíon was then known), with 40 spotlights indicating the main monuments, and wall displays devoted to historic Venetian buildings in the city. Also new is the Ceramics Room, illustrating how pottery has evolved over 15 centuries. Outstanding examples of Byzantine art include a 13th-century apse fresco, one of the earliest to survive on the island, depicting the Virgin, St John and the Church Fathers, Nicholas and Basil. One section is devoted to copies of frescoes from Cretan Byzantine churches, another contains liturgical objects from ancient churches now destroyed or converted to other uses.

El Greco El Greco's painting of the Monastery of Saint Catherine on Mount Sinai, the only painting by El Greco to remain on the island of his birth, is given place of honour in its own darkened and air-conditioned room. This is no great masterpiece, but it is instantly recognisable as belonging to a different world from the precise Byzantine icons and stylised frescoes that hang in the other rooms of the museum. There is an impressionistic quality about the brushwork: note the marvellous economy with which El Greco delineates the travelling Bedouin and his camel. The swirling yellow-pink clouds suggest some divine presence in the heavens and Mount Sinai seems to bend before an invisible wind. Altogether, the painting is suffused with a strange and unearthly light, suggestive of passion and emotion. The work betrays the influence of El Greco's teacher, Titian, who was himself one of the great Venetian masters who developed the use of light to heighten the drama of his paintings. El Greco – born in Iraklíon in 1541 and christened Doménico Theotokópoulos – painted this work around 1570, and it marks

a major stage in his transition from the Byzantine to the European style of art.

First floor Harrowing documentary photographs bring home the human heroism and tragedy of World War II and the Battle of Crete (*see pp104–5*). The most vivid shows Emmanuel Katsenavas and his son facing execution for their work in the Resistance – brave men visibly flinching in anticipation of the bullets that will shortly end their lives. Two contrasting studies have also been reconstructed here – one belonging to Emmanuel Tsouderós, the Réthymno-born prime minister of Greece at the time of the Battle of Crete, and the other to the writer Níkos Kazantzákis (*see p61*), along with a display of his novels in various editions and languages.

Folk art The cases devoted to Cretan folk art are full of richly coloured rugs and beautifully embroidered bodices and waistcoats. One room is furnished as a typical Cretan home, with a beaten-earth floor, stone benches and clay oil lamps. You can admire examples of Cretan bagpipes and lyres, and a splendid wedding bread, elaborately decorated with fishes and fruits.

Lysimáchou Kalokairinoú 7, opposite the Xenia Hotel, west of the Venetian Harbour. Tel: (2810) 288708. Open: summer Mon–Sat 9am–5pm; winter Tue–Sat 8.30am–3pm. Admission charge.

Agía Aikateríni (Icon Museum)

Crete holds a very special place in the history of icon painting. It was to this island that many of the best practitioners of the art fled after Constantinople (modern Istanbul) fell to the Ottomans in 1453. The Byzantine Empire had been deeply conservative in all things, including painting. Artists jealously preserved antique painting styles and techniques, which they brought to Crete and selectively passed on to pupils who were organised into schools and workshops, often attached to major monasteries.

East meets West The church and monastery of Agía Aikateríni, now the Icon Museum, was one of these schools. It was founded in 1555 when Crete was under Venetian rule. At almost precisely the same time, Venetian artists such as Titian, Veronese and Tintoretto were developing the High Renaissance style. Many Cretan artists studied for periods in Venetian workshops, and it was inevitable that there should be some cross-fertilisation between backward-looking Cretan icon painting and the Venetian avant-garde. El Greco (*see opposite*) was one product of the

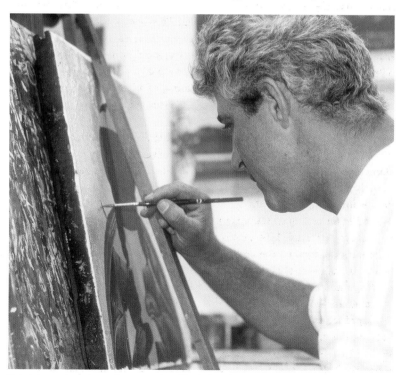

Today's icon painters keep alive a centuries-old artistic tradition

meeting of the two cultures, and another was his near contemporary, Mikhaíl Damaskinós, whose works form the highlight of this small museum. Little is known about the life of Damaskinós, except that he studied in Venice from 1577–82, and that the icons displayed here were painted after his return to Crete, probably in the 1590s, for the monastery at Vrontísiou (*see p62*).

Italian style The *Adoration of the Magi* by Damaskinós is an icon clearly influenced by Gozzoli's frescoes in the Medici Chapel in Florence. The lavish use of gold and the stylisation of the mountains and drapery mark this as a Byzantine work, but the figures, their gestures, expressions and postures, are far more realistic than is normal in the iconic style. From Botticelli's painting of the *Nativity*, Damaskinós has taken the idea of including himself in the picture; he is the crowned king in scarlet cloak, staring directly and questioningly out of the picture at the onlooker – in this case a somewhat idealised and youthful portrait. The icon depicting *The Last Supper* shows the degree to which Damaskinós embraced the rules of perspective, using the architectural framework and the table on which the supper is served to give his painting depth. His Apostles are all individual people, with thoughts, ideas and expressions of their own.

Back to Byzantine By comparison, the four remaining icons by Damaskinós show a reversion to the austerity and stylisation that is more typical of Byzantine icons. Faces are standardised and serenely emotionless. Several scenes are depicted at once, instead of the painting focusing on a single key event. In the *Virgin of the Burning Bush*, the central image is a symbolic one: the Virgin is burnt but not consumed, so she passes the test of absolute purity. *Noli me Tangere* shows the newly risen Christ appearing to the Holy Women, while *The Nicaean Ecumenical Council* shows the Church Fathers meeting to settle fundamental issues of Christian belief. The *Divine Liturgy* shows Christ as the first priest celebrating Communion with a congregation of angels.

Plateía Aikateríni. Tel: (2810) 288825. Open: summer daily 9.30am–7.30pm; winter Tue–Sun 8.30am–3pm. Admission charge.

ICONS AND MIRACLES

Icons are no mere pictures – to the faithful, they have miraculous powers, being a medium through which devotees can communicate with the saint or holy personage depicted – hence the votive offerings placed on or near icons by people seeking a cure for their complaints. Copies of miraculous icons have the same powers as the original – hence the practice of mass-producing icons and the innate conservatism of the art – worshippers want a precise copy, not artistic innovation. Perhaps that is why Damaskinós reverted to type in his later work – discarding all that he had learned from Renaissance artists.

Outside Iraklion
Agía Triáda
On the west side of the same hill on which Festós sits, there is another important Minoan site, Agía Triáda, traditionally described as a royal villa (for details of how to get there, *see p63*). Archaeologists are still not sure of the precise role of this building, or its relationship to Festós. It has been described as a rural retreat for the use of the Festós ruling family, and the very fine frescoes found here reinforce the idea that this was a place of leisured luxury. Also found here were the Chieftain Cup, Boxer Rhyton and Harvester Vase, the three famous stone vases, and the unique Agía Triáda Sarcophagus, all now in the Archaeological Museum, Iraklíon (*see pp29–32*).

The idyllic setting of the villa adds to the notion that it was built for pleasure, for the building sits on a slope with views towards the glistening Mesará Bay (Kolpos Mesaras). It may once have stood even closer to the sea, for there is evidence to suggest that waves once lapped the base of the hill; silt deposition has pushed the sea back considerably over the last three to four millennia.

Site tour Since the Minoan name of the villa is not known, Agía Triáda is named after a nearby church – but oddly enough, not the one that actually stands on the site: this church, Ágios Giórgios, nevertheless makes a good viewpoint from which to understand the site. Looking from the apse north to Mount Ida, the villa lies below, partly (*Cont. on p40*)

Agía Triáda: perhaps a summer palace or a cultural centre for sport, dance and song

Walk: Iraklíon

Despite its dusty streets and concrete buildings, Iraklíon remains a Cretan city at heart, with plenty of street life to make up for the uninspiring architecture (for map of route, see p27).

Allow 1½ hours.

Start at the Archaeological Museum. Walk around the western curve of Plateía Eleftherias.

1 Plateía Eleftherias

Pass the upmarket Astoria Capsis Hotel and several shops selling reproductions of Minoan pottery and jewellery. Irákliots still come to take coffee in the square, once the city's social heart, but huge tour buses calling at the museum have destroyed the former tranquillity. Turn right down Odós Daidálos to indulge in a spot of window-shopping. Smart boutiques and jewellery shops line both sides of the pedestrianised street.
Head northwest up Odós Daidálos and turn right on Odós 25 Avgoústou.

2 Plateía Venizélou

Plateía Venizélou is the city's other main square, lined with cafés, pastry shops and newspaper kiosks. The square is almost one large outdoor café and is liveliest at night. In the centre is Kríni Morozíni (the Morosini Fountain), built in 1628 by order of the city's Venetian governor, Francesco Morosini. The lower basin is carved with sea horses and cherubs, while the upper bowl rests on four lions, the lion being the symbol of St Mark and Venice.

Turn left here and cross the next road to find the city's bustling market in Odós 1866. This narrow street is lined with shops selling herbs, nuts, honey, embroidery, rugs, shoes, cheese, sponges and much more.

The fish market is at the very top of the street, where the aroma of coffee wafts from numerous cafés. One of these is set around a pretty six-sided kiosk converted from an old Turkish pumphouse, while behind is the Venetian Bembo Fountain of 1588 featuring a headless Roman statue from Ierápetra.

A walk through the fish market (in Odós Kartérou) introduces you to the many varieties of fish found in local waters – arrive early to see the stalls at their best.
Follow Odós Kartérou to Plateía Agía Aikateríni.

3 Plateía Agía Aikateríni ✦

The peaceful Plateía Agía Aikateríni has three churches. The biggest is the ornate 19th-century cathedral. More interesting is its small 16th-century predecessor, alongside, containing an intricately carved iconostasis (1759) and charming scenes depicting Adam and Eve. On the opposite side of the square, the church of St Catherine of Sinai (Agía Aikateríni) houses the Icon Museum (*see p35*). Follow the alley behind the church until it meets Odós 1821, then turn left back to Plateía Venizélou. Continue through the square, noting the Municipal Gallery on the right, housed in the church of Ágios Márcos, fronted by a 15th-century Renaissance arcade.

Almost next door is the Venetian armoury, now the town hall, fronted by a Venetian *loggia* (arcade) of 1626 decorated with military emblems. Behind is the church of Ágios Títos (St Titos), rebuilt in 1856, and housing the skull of the first bishop of Crete (*see p45*). The relic is not on display but is occasionally brought out to be shown to the faithful.

Odós 25 Avgoústou leads downhill from here to the harbour, and its imposing Venetian Fortress *Koúles* (*see p26*); the walk to the fortress and out along the sea wall is well worth doing for the views.

From Iraklíon's Venetian Fortress there are good views of the harbourside Arsenal and the city beyond

roofed over as a protection against rain. To the left are the private apartments, in the middle the storage areas, and to the right the public rooms for entertainment and ceremonies.

Beyond the villa is the main street of a small town. Shops, all identical in size and shape, line the right-hand side of the street, fronted by a row of column bases that once supported a colonnade, perhaps to shelter market stalls. The presence of these shops so close to the villa is one reason for questioning the theory that it was a royal residence. Perhaps the whole site was a centre for large seasonal gatherings of some kind – for sport, ritual, song and dance, maybe? Only further excavation will reveal the truth. What is not in doubt is the ferocity of the fire that destroyed this building in 1450 BC – fire-blackened floors and steps provide a vivid reminder of the final fate of the Minoan palace culture.

Agía Triáda is 64km (40 miles) southwest of Iraklíon.
Tel: (2810) 226470.
Open: summer daily 8am–8pm; winter daily 8.30am–3pm.
Admission charge.

Archánes

A good half day can be spent exploring the Minoan sites in and around Archánes, a prosperous agricultural town in the plain south of Iraklíon, renowned for the quality of its grapes. These are blessed in a festival that takes place every 6 August, following a custom that dates back, perhaps, to Minoan times, whereby the first fruits of the harvest are offered to the gods. Archánes is, in fact, two villages rather than one. Shortly after entering the first part, Páno Archánes, park in the main square with its walnut trees, shops, church and war memorial.

Archánes Archaeological Museum To learn more about the cemetery, it is worth visiting this excellent museum. Go back to the town, follow the one-way system until you reach a large café-lined square where you can park, and walk, following signs to the museum. One of the principal exhibits here is a vivid reconstruction of the so-called human-sacrifice shrine at Anemóspili, 3km (2 miles) northwest of Archánes. Here archaeologists found controversial evidence that the Minoans practised human sacrifice. In this case, a young man had been put to the knife in a last desperate attempt to avert the disastrous earthquake of 1700 BC which, minutes later, destroyed not just the shrine, but all the palaces on Crete, marking the end of the Old Palace period.
Open: Tue–Sun 8.30am–3pm.

Fourní Archaeologists cannot explore the palace site further because it lies beneath the modern town. They have, however, uncovered the huge cemetery at Fourní, on the town's outskirts. Reaching the site involves a long hard climb up a hill carpeted in wild flowers in spring.

Go back to the church and drive a short way out of the town, turn left by the large school and follow the signposted track until it ends; then follow the very steep track uphill to reach the site fence, following it to the left until you come to the entrance (normally open 8.30am–3pm).

Whether you think the effort of getting there worthwhile depends on your attitude to views. Set on a rocky plateau high above the town, the views stretch endlessly across the fertile plain that underpinned Minoan prosperity. The most impressive tomb on this site lies some distance to the left of the entrance. Tholos Tomb A has a ceremonial approach ramp leading to the narrow entrance of a huge beehive-shaped chamber which must once have been visible from all over the valley. Archaeologists found the undisturbed remains of a princess, still wearing her jewellery, here.

Minoan Archánes The scant remains of Minoan Archánes are not signposted, but are easy to find. Walk up the square, towards the fork where the one-way system begins. Take the left fork, then first left. Turn left at the end of the street, then right. The next track on the right will take you to the locked gates of the site where you can glimpse the massive blocks of well-shaped masonry forming the theatre area, archive and reservoir of a major Minoan palace. The stone has turned pink from the fierce heat of the fire that destroyed the palace in 1450 BC. Return to the main square, past houses built out of recycled Minoan masonry.

Panagía Vatiótissa church The little triple-naved church with its Baroque bell tower contains a surprisingly rich collection of icons, many dating from the 16th and 17th centuries. One shows the popular Cretan theme of the *Virgin as the Fount of Life* – the Virgin and Child stand in a fountain from which miracle-working waters flow.

The Baroque bell tower of Panagía Vatiótissa church in Archánes

Vineyards and olive groves dot the landscape at Vathýpetro

Vathýpetro Today the Anemóspili shrine is no more than a platform of stone (surrounded by a stinking landfill site), and not really worth a visit. Far more rewarding is the Minoan villa at Vathýpetro, 5km (3 miles) south of Archánes. This idyllic site is surrounded by vineyards, just as it was in the period 1700–1450 BC when the villa was in use. The state of preservation is outstanding – you can even visit the original wine-making room with its clay presses and pans set out as if ready for the grape harvest to begin.

Open: Tue–Sun 8.30am–3pm.

Archánes is 16km (10 miles) south of Iraklíon.

Festós

Minoan palace At the same time as Arthur Evans was excavating Knossós in 1900, an Italian team was busy uncovering the equally extensive remains of the Minoan palace at Festós. Evans's flair for self-publicity ensured that Knossós is now known the world over; far fewer people visit Festós. This magnificently sited palace is set on the flanks of a hill jutting out into the rich agricultural Mesarás plain. Archaeologists have argued convincingly that the palace was deliberately oriented so as to make the most of the views, and there is evidence here for gardens and water cascades, all of which must have contributed to the pleasure of living in such a fine spot.

Unlike Knossós, Festós has not been reconstructed, and at first sight can be confusing. There is a jumble of walls, wells and circular storage pits belonging to the Minoan town that clustered round the palace and cascaded down the slope of the hill to the plain below.

The path brings you down to the West Court, with its raised footpath. From here there are good views of the imposing **west façade** of the palace (3), aligned to face the setting sun. In fact, two façades are visible: the monumental staircase on the left and the massive walls to either side of it belong to the New Palace, built after the earthquake of 1700 BC. Running along the eastern edge of the West Court is the massive step-like plinth of the Old Palace façade, built around 1900 BC. Standing

Festós site plan

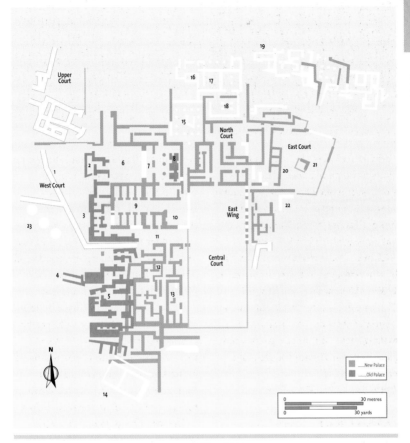

Upper Court

West Court

North Court

East Court

East Wing

Central Court

N

__New Palace
......Old Palace

| 0 | 30 metres |
| 0 | 30 yards |

KEY TO MAP

1 Theatre area
2 Shrine complex
3 West façade
4 Ramp
5 Shops
6 Grand stairway
7 Propylaeum
8 Lightwell
9 Storeroom block
10 Pillared hall
11 Corridor
12 Lustral basin
13 Pillar crypt
14 Temple of Rhea
15 Peristyle hall
16 Lustral basin
17 King's apartments
18 Queen's apartments
19 Archives
20 Workshops
21 Furnace
22 Colonnaded court
23 Storage pits (cisterns)

Symbol of wealth: oil storage jar

in the West Court it is clear that the remains of the Old Palace were levelled to create a platform on which the New Palace was erected. Archaeologists sometimes still work on the southern part of the site, uncovering more of the Old Palace and its associated town connected by a well-paved road. It is probable that valuable commodities such as oil and grain were carried in procession up this road to the palace, then brought up the **grand stairway** (6) to the palace storerooms.

The staircase leads to a lobby marked by the base of a massive circular **pillar** (7). Beyond the lobby are the remains of a triple-pillared entrance to a courtyard, or **lightwell** (8; a room open to the sky), from which narrow and winding passages lead left into the palace apartments and right into a massive **stores complex** (9).

Grain and oil were stored in large jars within the palace stores complex, the doors fastened with rope or cord to which a clay seal was attached to indicate ownership. Archaeologists found over 300 different seals, with designs ranging from animals to battle scenes and portraits. It is still not clear precisely how the Minoan economy worked, but the palace played an important role in the storage of valuable commodities – and perhaps in their distribution and export to mainland Greece, Egypt and Mesopotamia. It is possible that Minoans paid tax in the form of oil and grain – or that the ruling family was regarded as the owner of all the oil and grain produced by the community, or that individual owners entrusted their commodities to the palace for safekeeping.

The stores complex runs along the west flank of the large Central Court, aligned to make the most of northward views to Mount Ida – and specifically to the cave at Kamáres, which was an important focus of religious ritual during the Minoan era. To the north of the court, the narrow entrance to the private palace apartments is flanked by sentry boxes. This corridor was open to the sky – hence the drainage channel to carry rainwater away. The corridor leads to the North Court, to the right of which was once a small walled garden. To the north of the court, the **Royal Apartments** (17 and 18) also gave views – again to Mount Ida. On the far side of the Royal Quarters, down to the right, is a series of structures relating to the Old Palace, in one of which the famous and mysterious Festós disc (now in the Archaeological Museum, Iraklíon) was found. The disc, made of baked clay, is covered in indecipherable hieroglyphs arranged in a spiral pattern, perhaps of some religious significance.

Festós is 64km (40 miles) southwest of Iraklíon. Tel: (28920) 42315. Open: summer daily 8am–8pm; winter daily 8.30am–3pm. Admission charge.

Gortýs

When the Romans conquered Crete in 67 BC, the people of Gortýs took the side of the Roman general Quintus Metellus. As a reward, their city was made capital of the Roman province of Cyrenaica, which also encompassed parts of North Africa. By the time of the Roman conquest, Gortýs was already an ancient city, described by the ancient Greek historian Strabo as having a wall 10km (6 miles) long around it. It was comprehensively remodelled along typical Roman lines, with baths, theatres, a governor's palace and a forum. The site today is massive, but only a fraction has been excavated. The Roman remains lie scattered across a huge area, with fallen columns lying among vineyards and olive groves, and Roman brick and tile littering the ground. After Saracen raiders looted Gortýs in AD 824, it was simply abandoned and left to decay because of the difficulty of defending the site.

Ágios Títos (Church of St Titus) One building stands remarkably intact: the Church of St Titus dominates the entrance to the site with its massive apse standing to the roof. The church dates back to the 6th century, and is the burial place of St Titus, the first bishop of Crete. Titus was sent here on a successful mission to convert Crete to Christianity after St Paul had visited the island in AD 50. It is quite likely that Titus would have made Gortýs his base, since it was then the largest city on Crete, with a population of approximately 30,000.

The 6th-century AD Ágios Títos church

The 7th-century BC Temple of Apollo Pythios, with its stepped altar

Odeon – The Law Code of Gortýs
Emerging from what would have been
the west door of the church of St Titus,
you can see, over to the right, the
impressive remains of the 1st-century
BC Odeon, a theatre built for music and
poetry recitals. The modern brick
structure to the rear of the theatre
shelters a remarkable 10m (33ft) stretch
of wall covered in ancient Greek script,
recording the Laws of Gortýs. Much of
what we know about early Greek life
and society comes from this important
document, carved in sandstone, and
found among the foundations of a
pre-Roman building on the site of
the Odeon.

The inscription reads from left to
right and from right to left on alternate
lines, in a style known as
boustrophedon, meaning 'like the
pattern made by oxen ploughing a

field'. Though the inscription dates to
around 450 BC, it probably records laws
that had been observed for generations
before – indeed, Plato, who mentions
the code in his own book of Laws,
describes it as a very conservative code.
It divides the inhabitants of Gortýs into
four classes – rulers, freemen, serfs and
slaves – and describes in detail the
rights of each with regard to property
ownership, inheritance, marriage,
divorce and the adoption of children,
as well as laying down appropriate
penalties for crimes such as rape,
adultery and assault.

Temples and palaces More excavated
remains lie on the opposite side of the
road. Turn left (east) along the Iraklíon
road and walk for some 300m (330yds),
ignoring the right turn to Mitrópoli.
Look for a paved track on the right-

hand side of the road that leads down to the Temple of Isis and Serapis, built in the 1st century AD for the worship of these Egyptian gods. To the south is the Temple of Apollo Pythios, a fascinating structure that may have been constructed as early as the 7th century BC and served as the main temple of the Roman city.

A track skirts the massive palace complex of the Roman provincial governor – the ruler of Crete and much of North Africa, responsible for ensuring a steady flow of wheat from these territories to other parts of the Roman Empire. Through the site fence it is possible to see beautifully paved courtyards, headless statues, fallen columns and numerous walls.

Tel: (28920) 31144. The area enclosing the church of St Titus and the Odeon is open: summer daily 8am–8pm; winter daily 8.30am–3pm. Admission charge. The rest of the site lies in olive groves and is freely accessible.

Gortýs is 46km (29 miles) south of Iraklíon, and 16km (10 miles) east of Festós.

Eastern Crete

The restored North Entrance of Knossós (*see p50*)

Byzantine churches

In AD 293 the Roman Empire, now so large that it covered almost all of modern Europe and the Near East, was split, for ease of administration, into eastern and western divisions. From AD 330 the Eastern Empire began to grow in stature when Constantine the Great founded the new city of Constantinopolis (modern Istanbul) on the site of a former Greek colony called Byzantium.

From Byzantium came the name for a new style of art and architecture that started here when the Church of the Apostles (now Ayía Sophia) was built in 537. Characterised by round arches, circles, domes and rich mosaic work (from which fresco later developed), this style became the norm for church architecture in the Eastern Empire and beyond, lasting right up to the present.

The churches of Crete

Crete has one surviving church from the early Byzantine period – the 6th-century Ágios Títos, at Gortýs (see p45). By contrast, there are several hundred churches and monasteries from the 10th to the 17th century, surviving in various states of repair. Some of the finest and most important have been restored, but most remain untouched, their frescoes cracked and blackened by centuries of candle soot, their simple walls leaning this way and that.

Most are simple churches with a nave, dome and apse. Separating the nave from the apse is an iconostasis, a carved and often gilded wooden screen on which icons (see p36) are displayed. The iconostasis serves to screen the altar, since, in the Orthodox liturgy, key moments such

Today's churches continue to be built in a simple style

The Byzantine church at Episkopí is one of the oldest churches in Greece

as the mystic transformation of bread and wine into Christ's flesh and blood are performed in secret, away from the eyes of the congregation. Larger churches may have a second or even a third nave, each with its own iconostasis and apse, and occasionally a narthex, an entrance vestibule running the width of the church at the western end.

Frescoes

Frescoes are closely related to the architecture of the church. The dome, which represents the heavens, is usually painted with the figure of Christ Pantocrator (Ruler of All) looking down on the congregation, his hands raised in blessing and to display the wounds of his Crucifixion. In smaller churches without domes, Christ Pantocrator appears in the apse instead. In larger churches, the apse may feature the Last Supper, with Christ in the centre, or more probably the Communion of the Saints, with Christ as the officiating priest surrounded by angels, saints and patriarchs.

Many frescoes are also dated by an inscription, often located in the apse, or at the rear of the church, on the west wall. Occasionally, there will also be a portrait of the donor and his family – look for this by the west door, or at the western end of the north wall of the nave.

KEY TO MAP

1	Walled pits	24	Corridor of the draughts board
2	West Porch	25	Northeast hall
3	Corridor of the Procession Fresco	26	Magazine of the Giant Pithoi
4	South Propylaea	27	East bastion
5	Staircase to the piano nobile	28	Court of the stork spout
6	Lower storeroom block	29	Craftsman's workshop
7	Pillar crypts	30	East portico
8	Room of the column bases	31	Medallion room
9	Room of the tall pithos	32	Corridor of the bays
10	Temple repository	33	East–west corridor
11	Vat room	34	Grand staircase
12	Antechamber	35	Hall of the colonnades
13	Throne room	36	Hall of the double axes
14	Inner sanctum		(King's megaron)
15	Lower long corridor	37	Queen's megaron
16	Deposit of tablets	38	Bathroom
17	Lustral basin	39	Lavatory
18	Royal Road	40	Court of the distaffs
19	Theatre area	41	Shrine of the double axes
20	Old keep	42	Corridor of sword tablets
21	Northwest portico	43	House of chancel screen
22	North entrance passage with	44	Minoan kiln
	Charging Bull fresco	45	House of the fallen blocks
23	Pillar hall (customs house)	46	House of sacrificed oxen

Knossós

Knossós is one of the world's most famous archaeological sites and in high season it swarms with visitors. In summer it is open for long hours, and a visit over lunchtime or in the early evening may prove more enjoyable than a morning visit when the crowds are at their peak. Allow at least two hours for your visit. (*See plan opposite.*)

The palace The present palace at Knossós is the last in a series of buildings on the site that date back to the origins of civilisation on Crete. Beneath the palace, archaeologists have discovered the remains of a Neolithic settlement, dating to around 6000 BC. The earliest palace on the site dates from around 2000 BC. This, like all the other palaces on Crete, was destroyed in the earthquake of 1700 BC and then rebuilt in its present form.

Today, despite the collapse of the upper storeys of the palace, which were built of timber, stone and plaster, it is still possible to gauge something of its vast and labyrinthine nature. At its height, the palace and its town spread over 75ha (185 acres) and had a population of around 12,000 – the same as Iraklíon in the Middle Ages.

Unlike the other palaces of Crete, Knossós was only partially damaged by fire in 1400 BC. Indeed, it has been

Knossós site plan

inhabited continuously ever since, and the present villages of Knossós and Makritíchos (meaning 'long wall') lie on top of the Minoan town.

Even so, the site has been preserved in a remarkable state: wonderful treasures, such as the gaming board and the statue of the Snake Goddess, now in the Archaeological Museum in Iraklíon, along with bronze vessels, stone jars and the throne itself, were all found where they had been left. This suggests that, for centuries after the end of Minoan civilisation, the site was respected and not robbed – perhaps because of powerful memories of the myth of the Minotaur,

the bull-headed monster of the labyrinth, who was thought to dwell beneath the palace.

Visitors to the site are greeted by a bust of Arthur Evans (*see pp56–7*) who excavated Knossós between 1900 and 1906. The bust stands at the entrance to the West Court and, to the left, there are three huge stone-lined pits (1), probably built as granaries. At the base of the central pit you can see the steps and stone walls of one of the oldest stone houses found on the site, built around 2000 BC.

The whole of the palace complex served a ceremonial purpose, and the

Pithoi in the palace storerooms

raised paths that cross the West Court were built as processional ways. Follow the raised path to the right of the Court and you will come up to the roped-off palace façade, clad in huge blocks of gypsum. This light and easily carved stone was used throughout the palace for cladding and paving. The use of gypsum for the façade would have given the palace a gleaming white, marble-like appearance.

To the right of the façade is the **West Porch** (2), marked by a single central column base. Imagine now that massive double doors lie ahead. These swing open as we enter the **Corridor of the Procession Fresco** (3), so-called because the walls were lined on both sides with a frieze depicting hundreds of life-sized youths and maidens in procession and playing music.

The floor, still intact, is paved with sheets of blue schist set in red mortar. The corridor ends abruptly because the hillside has fallen away at this point; it once ran around three sides of a rectangle to return to the Central Court of the palace. To get there, turn left, then right through a reconstructed doorway into the paved area known as the **South Propylaea** (4). The pillared entrance to the palace is decorated with a copy of the Cup Bearer Fresco, one of the best preserved of the figures from the Procession Fresco. Looking back, note the tapered red-painted wooden columns that support the reconstructed doorways of the palace. The Minoans used whole trees as pillars, but inverted them, so that the wider root end of the tress was at the top.

Beyond the fresco, the **staircase** ahead (5) leads to an area of the palace completely reconstructed by the excavator, Arthur Evans. It was his theory that the main reception rooms of the palace lay on this well-lit and airy upper storey. As you cross the upper floor, there are views to the left down on to the palace storerooms. Here you can see clearly the *pithoi*, giant storage jars, lining the long walls of each room, and then cisterns dug into the floor of the central corridor to create more storage space. We know, from Linear B clay tablets, that oil, grain, wool, dyestuffs and textiles were stored in rooms such as these, representing very considerable wealth.

Straight ahead lies a gallery where reproductions of the most famous Knossós frescoes have been hung, and through this room you reach a terrace. Turn left and left again to find a little staircase – one of many that must have provided a short cut from one part of the labyrinthine palace to another. Of equal interest is the fact that the walls containing the staircase are built on foundations from the Old Palace – hence its unusual rounded shape.

The staircase brings you down to the Central Court, with the palace throne room on the left. In the **antechamber** (12) is a reconstruction of what Evans called 'the oldest throne in the world' – while the original gypsum throne survives intact, standing where it was placed some 3,500 years ago, in the railed-off **inner sanctum** (14). This throne room was in disarray when Evans excavated it, with jars overturned and littering the floor – enough for him to suggest that some dramatic final event took place here.

Minoan murals adorn the inner walls of the Central Court

On the opposite side of the Central Court are the **Royal Apartments**. This suite contains the most gracious rooms in the palace, many of them decorated with fine frescoes, such as the Dolphin and the Girl Dancer. Originally reconstructed by Evans as bedrooms, bathrooms and dressing rooms, it is now thought more likely that they were shrines, and not domestic rooms of any sort at all.

Continuing to the north of the site, there is a roofed-over area known as the **Magazine of the Giant Pithoi** (26), part of the room dating to the Old Palace period, and therefore almost 4,000 years old. Just in front of the magazine, steps descend right down to the palace east entrance. Lining the staircase is a little water channel, with miniature rills (furrows to make the water ripple as it flows) and cascades. Anyone entering the palace on this side would have been greeted by the gentle sound of running water. Returning past the giant *pithoi*, to the top of the steps straight ahead, you reach a paved area with floor grilles: here are terracotta pipes from the original palace water supply, and stone drainage channels to carry rainwater away. A covered room to the left is known as the **Medallion room** (31) because of the medallion-like circles applied as decoration to the giant storage jars found here. A staircase alongside brings you back to the Central Court.

The north side of the Central Court is dominated by the imposing reproduction of the **Charging Bull Fresco** (22). Anyone entering the palace from the north side would have been greeted by this intimidating fresco, thought to have been part of a larger bull-leaping frieze. To the west of this can be seen a reconstructed **lustral basin** (17), consisting of steps leading down to the area where visitors were expected to wash and anoint themselves with oil.

Going west again is a **theatre area** enclosed on two sides by steps (19). These have been interpreted as seating for the audience at some kind of sport or ritual, but alternative theories abound – more plausible is the idea that important guests were greeted here and, perhaps, entertained, before proceeding to the lustral basin for anointing and washing and from there on into the palace. This explanation seems correct in view of the fact that the theatre area stands at the end of the so-called **Royal Road** (18). This wide and well-paved street connects the palace with the vast town that once surrounded it and with Festós to the south. It has the distinction of being the oldest paved road in Europe.

Knossós, tel: (2810) 231940, is 5km (3 miles) south of Iraklíon. Open: summer daily 8am–8pm; winter 8.30am–3pm.
Admission charge.

The palace of Knossós is part of Crete's early history

Arthur Evans

Arthur John Evans was born in 1851, the son of Sir John Evans, a paper manufacturer and amateur archaeologist of Welsh descent. His father's interest became a passion with him, and he was largely responsible for the excavations of the capital of the Minoan civilisation, which he not only discovered, but substantially reconstructed.

A bust of Sir Arthur John Evans features prominently at the entrance to Knossós, paying tribute to a man who is something of a hero to the Cretans, as he should be, given how much Knossós earns in tourist revenue. Evans is less of a hero to the archaeological establishment, criticised for his intuitive reconstruction of frescoes and rooms in the palace: Logan Pearsall Smith, in a letter to Bernhard Berenson, wrote in 1926 that 'Evans is repainting and reconstructing Knossós in a gaudy style of bad taste which gives it something of the look of his hideous house in Boar's Hill'.

Controversial figure

Few visitors today would agree with this harsh judgement, but it remains fashionable to find fault with Evans'

theories and interpretations, just as it was in his own time.

Evans sometimes invited criticism because of his own strength of character and his possessive attitude to all things Minoan. He was, after all, the owner of Knossós, having purchased the site in 1894, and used his own private fortune to fund the excavations. Ownership of the site was conveyed to the British School at Athens in 1924, and was then transferred to the Greek government in 1952.

The discovery of the Minoans

Evans began digging in 1900, making sensational discoveries of art and literature almost every day, discoveries that were reported with astonishment in newspapers all over Europe, as the history of the ancient world was completely rewritten.

Linear A and B

Evans' name has become inextricably linked with the Minoans, but many other archaeologists have worked on the island, and continue to do so. The palace of Zákros was only discovered in 1961 and several sites are under excavation now, including the

Arthur Evans with finds from the Knossós palace

peripheral areas at Knossós. This work has added immensely to our knowledge of the Minoans, but their language and script – known as Linear A – have not yet been fully deciphered, despite enormous efforts on the part of many scholars. Linear A was in use from around 1650 BC but was superseded, after the final destruction of the New Palaces in 1450 BC, by the Mycenaean-influenced Linear B – a script that has been deciphered, yielding a great deal of information about the Minoan economy, but at a time when Minoan civilisation was a shadow of its former glory.

Abiding mysteries

The other great unsolved mystery is the precise cause of the fires that destroyed the Minoan palaces in 1450 BC. Evans' theory that the eruption of Théra, a whole half century earlier, caused the calamity is no longer believed. Many alternative theories exist, none of them borne out by the evidence – but there is increasing support for the idea that a major exodus occurred after 1450 BC, with the Minoans, expert seafarers, fleeing their island and migrating all over Europe to found new cultures. The Etruscans of ancient Italy and the Philistines of ancient Palestine are among the peoples whose ceramics, jewellery and bronzework bear a striking and intriguing similarity to that of the Minoans. Evans was knighted for his services to archaeology. He died in 1941.

Mália

Mália is the capital of beach-holiday Crete, a small town that has been swamped by discos, Irish bars, English-style pubs and tavernas that sell beefburgers, English breakfasts and roasts on Sunday rather than Cretan food. The reason for all this development is the fine sandy beach that spreads for some distance either side of the town. Despite its size, this beach can be very crowded, and there are more atmospheric places to swim, one of them being just 4km (2½ miles) east of Mália, alongside the Minoan palace remains. To the disco-hungry crowd who come to Mália, the fact that there is a major Minoan palace on the town's doorstep is probably a matter of supreme indifference, which helps to explain why so few people visit the excavated remains and beach nearby.

Palace This sits on the coastal plain within sight and sound of the sea, and bumps in the fields to the south indicate the presence of a large town, as yet little explored. French-run excavations are continuing, and informative displays are found at key points around the site, explaining the work in progress.

A striking feature of the palace is the sheer number of areas set aside for storage. Sunken clay-lined pits and barrack-like blocks, built from mud

Silent reminders of the Mália Palace

brick and with their wine and oil-storage jars intact, surround the central court, leaving only a small area designated as living accommodation. To the northwest of the palace (in the area known as Quartier M), archaeologists have uncovered a group of buildings used as the palace administration block. Clay tablets inscribed with inventorial data, and seal stones used to seal boxes, jars and doorways, have been found here in great quantity. As with other Minoan palace sites, the building clearly played a key role in the storage and distribution of goods, but we are no nearer to knowing whether Minoan society was authoritarian, with all resources owned and controlled by the ruling family, or whether it was based on a more benign system of communal ownership.
Tel: (28970) 31597. Palace open: Tue–Sun 8.30am–3pm. Closed: Mon. Admission charge.

Mália is 38km (24 miles) east of Iraklíon.

Mália environs
Káto Karouzaná Káto Karouzaná bills itself as 'The Traditional Village'. Popular with coach tours, the village is really an excuse to persuade visitors to part with their money in return for handicrafts such as woven rugs and pottery (although woven and painted by hand, the designs are not always traditional). Displays of Greek dancing and music are put on in the evening, and used by tour companies.
15km (9 miles) south of Chersonísou.

Lychnostatis Museum This is located just off the National Highway to the east of Chersonísou, another busy package-tour resort, some 12km (7 miles) to the west of Mália. Guided tours take in a reconstructed Cretan house, windmill, shepherd's shelter, pottery, weaving workshops and an olive oil press. Wine tastings and an audiovisual introduction to the attractions of Crete are all part of the package.
Open: Sun–Fri 9am–2pm. Closed: Sat. Admission charge.

Mílatos This attractive fishing village is set above a pretty pebble beach. Mílatos is mentioned by Homer as one of the Cretan towns that sent troops to fight in the Trojan War, and archaeological evidence suggests that the village has been continually occupied for at least 5,000 years. Legend has it that migrants from this village founded the great and famous city of Miletos on the modern Turkish coast. Though this may seem no more than a coincidence of names, archaeologists have, in fact, found Minoan settlement remains at Turkish Miletos. About 3km (2 miles) east of the village lies the cave of Mílatos, where in 1823 an estimated 3,000 Cretans taking refuge were besieged by the Ottomans. Forced to surrender and promised a safe passage, they were then massacred or taken as slaves. A chapel with a small ossuary commemorates the event.
10km (6 miles) east of Mália.

Mátala

Even if you are not a beach lover, Mátala's sheltered bay, sandstone cliffs and lovely sunset views will not leave you unmoved. Mátala also makes an excellent base for exploring the major archaeological sites of Festós and Gortýs. The beach is impeccably clean and local shops are very well stocked, as befits a village that has almost become a German colony (there are even fragments of the Berlin Wall hanging in the reception area of one hotel).

Archaeology The cliffs to the north of the bay contain scores of man-made caves where hippies made their homes when Crete was first 'discovered' in the 1970s. The caves were originally excavated in the 2nd century BC to serve as rock-cut tombs, and some have ornate carved niches within. Today the caves are fenced off.

A little to the north of Mátala is another sandy beach, stretching south from Kalamáki to Kommós. Kommós is the site of the Minoan harbour that served Festós, and American archaeologists digging here in the last ten years have uncovered substantial remains of roads, warehouses, dry docks and temples, some of which can be seen through the site fence.

Mátala is completely closed, like a ghost town, from November to March.

Mátala is 70km (43 miles) southwest of Iraklíon, 10km (6 miles) southwest of Festós.

The striking rock-cut tombs of Mátala were once used as homes

Mátala's west-facing bay is the ideal place to watch the sun go down

Myrtía

Kazantzákis Museum Níkos Kazantzákis is one of the few Cretans whose name is well known beyond the shores of his own island, though his fame owes much more to film versions of his work than to his actual writings. The Kazantzákis Museum in Myrtía attempts to fill out the very vague picture that most of us have of his life and work. The museum is located on the village square in what is claimed to be the house of Kazantzákis' father. In fact, it has been substantially extended to accommodate case after case of Kazantzákis memorabilia: books, stills from film and stage versions of his works, costume designs, and personal possessions such as signet rings and fountain pens.

Kazantzákis (1883–1957) was born in Iraklíon and studied law at Athens University and political science in Paris. Fellow Cretan Eleftherias Venizélos (*see p106*) made Kazantzákis Minister of Welfare in his Greek government of 1919, but he preferred travelling to politics, and lived abroad for many years writing a series of poems, plays, stories and poetic dramas. His grandiose language is out of fashion now, and his work is little read or performed.

Controversial novels Kazantzákis became widely known through the enormous success of *Zorba the Greek* (1946), which was turned into a popular

(*Cont. on p64*)

CRETAN LIARS

On the way up to Myrtía look out for the distinctive profile of Mount Yioúktas to the west (right) once past Knossós. The mountain, with its radar station, looks like a human face, with prominent brow, nose, lips and chin. Cretans have long believed that this is the face of Zeus who lies buried beneath the mountain. Other Greeks branded Cretans as liars for daring to suggest that Zeus was anything but immortal (*see pp81–2*).

Tour: Cretan archaeology

This route takes in some of Crete's star archaeological attractions – the Roman capital of Gortýs and the Minoan palaces of Festós and Agía Triáda, ending up on the beautiful beach of Mátala.

Allow all day for the tour (with an early start) and consider spending the night in Mátala, then driving on to Agía Galíni to take the Amári Valley tour (see pp134–5) in the reverse direction to Réthymno.

1 Giofyros Valley
Take the westward road out of Iraklíon, following signs to Réthymno. At the Old Road/New Road junction, around 5km (3 miles) out of town, turn left. Be sure to pass under the highway rather than joining the sliproad. From here on it is easy driving through the picturesque Giofyros Valley to Gortýs.

A medieval Cretan icon

For a two-day trip, branch off in Agía Varvára to visit Zarós and its churches. *Continue on or turn right in Agía Varvára at the junction signposted to Zarós.*

2 Agía Varvára and Zarós
These scenic flower-filled villages make a pleasant stop en route to the Moní Vrontísiou. Sample the spring waters in Zarós for which the village is renowned. *Continue through the village, turn right and after 2km (1¼ miles) turn up a road signposted to the monastery.*

3 Moní Vrontísiou
Situated high on a hilltop overlooking the fertile Mesarás plain, the Moní Vrontísiou (*see p66*) is a splendid monastery and known for its colourful frescoes and panoramic views. *Now return to the main road, turn right and head for Voríza.*

4 Varsamónero
Halfway through Voríza a blue sign points to the church of Varsamónero.

The simple church (*see p66*) and its peaceful setting are worth the diversion. *Return to Zarós and just before leaving the village turn right (signposted Moíres). This fast new road leads to Kapparianá. Look out for the left turn to Gortýs.*

5 Gortýs

Gortýs (*see p45*) is the ancient Roman capital of Crete. It is tempting to explore this fascinating site for hours, but bear in mind Agía Triáda shuts at 3pm. *Drive west (signposted Vóroi) for 14km (9 miles) and then take the left turn signposted to Festós.*

6 Festós

The sprawling site of Festós (*see p42*) is one of the most important archaeological sites in the world. *Turn right immediately beyond the end of the car park (opposite the little church) for your journey to Agía Triáda.*

7 Agía Triáda

Travel for around 3km (2 miles) along the track, which winds its way through countryside. You'll find Agía Triáda just below you to your left behind a forest of pine trees (*see p37*). *Return to Festós and turn right for Mátala.*

8 Mátala

Mátala (*see p60*) makes a relaxing end to the day's excursion. If you are staying over, find a west-facing café by sunset to watch the sun go down in a blaze of colour.

Tour: Cretan archaeology

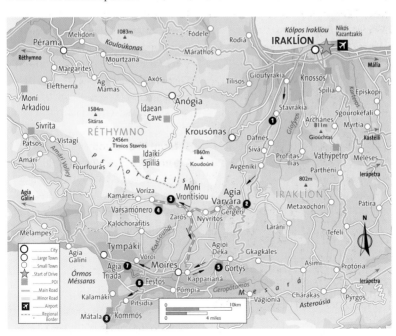

film with a haunting theme tune starring Anthony Quinn and Alan Bates (1964). Controversy also helped to promote his name: *Freedom or Death* (1953), about the Cretan resistance to Ottoman rule, and *The Last Temptation of Christ* (1954) were both condemned by the Roman Catholic Church for blasphemy. More recently, Martin Scorsese's film version of *The Last Temptation of Christ* ran into similar trouble, criticised for portraying Christ as flawed and truly human, rather than sinless and divine. Conspiracy theorists go so far as to claim that the Church prevented Kazantzákis from receiving the Nobel Prize for Literature when he was nominated in 1955.
Tel: (2810) 742451. Museum open: summer Tue–Sun 8am–8pm; winter Tue–Sun 8.30am–3pm.

Myrtía is 16km (10 miles) southeast of Iraklíon, 11km (7 miles) southeast of Knossós.

Vóroi
Museum of Cretan Ethnology The area around Festós, in southern Crete, is well worth visiting for its major archaeological sites; another incentive to come here is the excellent Museum of Cretan Ethnology in Vóroi. This modern and sophisticated museum is housed in a building just to the south of the church.

The displays here will answer a lot of the questions that any inquisitive traveller on Crete will have at the back of their minds. For example, what are the plants that the little old ladies, clad in black, are foraging for when you see them scouring the wild rocky hillsides of Crete. Case Number 1 provides some answers and covers the theme of foods gathered in the wild, from freshwater crabs and snails, to wild 'greens' (*horta* in Greek) – plants picked from the hillsides at any time from autumn until late spring and cooked by boiling or frying in oil. The ingredients of *horta* include many relatives of the dandelion, as well as wild asparagus and artichoke. Once, such wild foods were a vital supplement to a near-starvation diet – today they are soul food for Cretans, evoking memories of the simple life of their forefathers, and the little old ladies sell the results of their foraging in local markets or to tavernas.

The next run of display cases deals with the farming year on Crete, showing and explaining the various tools that are used at every stage, from tilling the soil, to grinding wheat using watermills or hand querns. The exhibits include a vicious-looking plank set with sawblades and flints, resembling a medieval instrument of torture, but actually used for threshing grain. The operator stood or sat on the board while the animal pulled it round the threshing floor, the flint chips and saw blades breaking open the ears of wheat to release the grain. This, and the various ox-ploughs and sickles on display, are of a type that is quite likely to have been in use in the Mediterranean area from Neolithic times until as recently as the 1970s and 1980s. Equally informative displays cover olive oil production, viticulture and animal husbandry.

The enormous importance of sheep and goats to the Cretan economy is underlined by the displays on milk and cheese making, these two foods having provided the main source of protein in the Cretan diet for centuries. Meat was a rare luxury – sheep were kept principally for milk and wool, and cattle served primarily as draught animals; hens and pigeons supplied eggs; and rabbits and pigs were bred for meat. This diet was supplemented by hare, partridge and rabbit, trapped in the wild and once abundant on Crete.

The ingenuity of Cretan potters is illustrated in the section on household vessels: jars for storing honey have a water trap around the rim to keep out ants and there are purpose-made vessels for storing smoked and pickled meat,

salted fish, olives, oil, cereals, rusks, salt, water and wine – once the staples of the Cretan diet. Equally varied is the range of baskets (25 different types) used for fishing, harvesting and foraging, with marked regional variations in size and shape. Some baskets were used for storing grain, the inside having first been coated with cow-dung plaster and whitewash to deter weevils and mice. Pungent herbs were also placed among the grain to prevent meal worm developing.

The museum's most colourful displays cover the processes involved in converting raw wool into richly patterned cloth. Wonderful examples of bags, towels, aprons, blankets and saddle covers are displayed, the likes of which are very rarely seen for sale in Crete today. Modern weavers still use the Cretan handloom, but their bright chemical dyes and leaping dolphin motifs are designed to please tourists –

Bright weaves typical of the exhibits at the Museum of Cretan Ethnology, Vóroi

few now produce the traditional striped and geometric fabrics, in rich reds, greens and yellows obtained from vegetable dyes.
Museum of Cretan Ethnology. Tel: (28920) 91110. Open: daily 8.30am–3pm. Admission charge.

Vóroi is 60km (37 miles) southwest of Iraklíon, 3km (2 miles) north of Festós.

Zarós

The large village of Zarós is set high on the southern foothills of the Psiloreítis range of mountains and is surrounded by a cluster of worthwhile churches and monasteries. The reason for Zarós being located where it is becomes apparent if you stop for a coffee in the village and explore the pretty side streets, with their colourful displays of pot plants. Water is abundant here, running down the sides of the streets and splashing into stone troughs – numerous springs discharge from the hills behind the village, and in Roman times these were channelled into an artificial watercourse and carried to the town of Gortýs, some 13km (8 miles) south.
Zarós is 54km (34 miles) southwest of Iraklíon.
Churches open all day (often closed in winter). Free admission.

Zarós environs
Moní Vrontísiou To find Vrontísiou monastery, continue through Zarós, turning right about 2km (1¼ miles) west of the village. The monastery

entrance is shaded by two giant plane trees, and to the left is a small Venetian-era fountain featuring the now headless figures of Adam and Eve. Below them, water gushes from the mouths of wild creatures with flowing locks – possibly intended as lions. The fountain probably dates from the 15th century, while the monastery itself was founded a century earlier, and dedicated to St Antony, patron saint of hermits. The double-naved church is full of ancient icons, though the most famous, painted by the great Mikhaíl Damaskinós, are now in the Icon Museum in Iraklíon (*see p35*). The right-hand (southern) nave preserves darkened 14th-century frescoes, depicting the Last Supper (in the apse) and scores of venerable saints and patriarchs, representing the Communion of the Saints, along the walls. Coming out of the church, do not miss the splendid views over the Mesarás Plain to be had from the terrace.

Varsamónero
To reach Varsamónero from Moní Vrontísiou return to the main road and turn right, continuing to Voríza. Halfway up the hill in the middle of this village, look for a blue sign pointing left to Varsamónero. The bumpy concrete road gives way eventually to a dirt track, which leads for 2.5km (1½ miles) to the church. This is set in a peaceful spot alone among the hills. The exterior is very simple – it has been cited as an example of Venetian influence on Byzantine

architecture, but this runs to little more than a hint of Gothic dogtooth decoration and a carved Venetian coat of arms over the westernmost door.

This door, as becomes apparent when you step into the church, leads into a narthex, or antechamber to the main body of the double-naved church. The whole of the interior is covered in richly coloured frescoes. The oldest are in the northern nave; dating to 1321, they depict the life of the Virgin. Within the lovely iconostasis (the wooden screen carved with vine-leaves that separates the nave from the apse), there are scenes from the Life of Christ, including his Baptism and Ascension, and his Entombment and Resurrection.

In the southern nave, the frescoes, painted in 1406–7, depict scenes from the life of John the Baptist. Directly opposite the entrance door is the scene in which Salome dances for Herod, while his guests tuck into a sumptuous banquet. In the next scene to the left, John the Baptist is beheaded. On the pillar behind these two scenes, the elongated figure of John the Baptist with long and straggly hair has been compared to the work of El Greco.

In the third part of the church, there is a little apse set into the southeastern wall. The frescoes here, painted around 1431, depict Christ celebrating communion surrounded by a heavenly host of saints and angels. The remaining frescoes depict the exploits of the soldier-saint Phanourios, to whom this church is dedicated. On the opposite wall there are several further scenes from the life of Christ, and a scene in which demons are being spewed out of the mouth of a demented man.

Visitors to Varsamónero's fresco-covered church will be enchanted by its rural setting

LASSÍTHIOU PROVINCE
Lassíthiou

The Lassíthiou, also known as the Lasíthi Plain, is a large oval plateau, completely ringed by mountains, with some 17 small villages dotted around its rim. The villagers make their living from agriculture: apples, almonds and potatoes are the principal crops, and the plain is beautiful in spring when the fruit trees are in blossom. In summer, the fields are irrigated using hundreds of white-sailed windmills, which draw water up from underground aquifers (for a suggested route, *see pp70–71*). The windmills are a famous and picturesque tourist attraction, though it can be hit and miss whether any will be operating at the time of your visit.

The aquifers (underground reservoirs) are restocked by the heavy rains and snow that fall from October onwards. Flooding would be a threat if it were not for the drainage channels that divide the plain up into a grid, resembling the squares on a chessboard. The drainage system was first installed by the Romans, but the present system, cleaned out and restored, was installed under Venetian rule.

Caves and farmhouses

Most visitors come to Lassíthiou for the Díktaean Cave at Psychró (*see pp80–81*). A less crowded alternative is the Trapéza (or Krónio) Cave, to the south of Tzermiádho. This was used for burials in the Neolithic era (around 5000 BC) and later as a Minoan sanctuary.

Also well worth a visit is the **Folk Museum** alongside the church in the village of Ágios Giórgios. This occupies a genuine farmhouse, with low ceilings, and smoke-blackened beams, built in 1800. Beside the door is a loom and the family bed is built over the wine press. Simple handmade furniture is stacked against the walls, and the kitchen area has a quern for grinding wheat, a bread oven, kneading troughs and storage jars. Alongside is a byre for sheep and goats and a separate stable for donkeys, with saddles, panniers and ploughs of the working farm. A more spacious and modern house next door shows how Cretans live today.

Folk Museum open: summer only, daily 10am–4pm.

Lassíthiou lies 60km (37 miles) southeast of Iraklíon, 21km (13 miles) south of Mália.

Lassíthiou's canvas-sailed windmills draw water from underground reservoirs

Ágios Nikólaos

Ágios Nikólaos is one of the busiest towns on Crete during summer. It is a lively university town with a lovely laid-back vibe about the place for most of the year.

Archaeological Museum

The town's archaeological museum is just out of the centre, on the steep Odós Konstantinou Paleológou. Here the origins of Minoan culture are particularly well represented, with good examples of Neolithic and pre-Palatial Minoan material on display in Room 1. Note the elegantly burnished vases with their long spouts and the stone phallus-shaped idol from a remote cave in Eastern Crete. The fertility theme continues in Room 2, where the so-called Goddess of Mýrtos is displayed, a bizarre early Minoan clay libation vase with phallic neck and head, clay lumps for breasts and a hatched triangle of pubic hair. She is less appealing than the delicate vessels made from marble and other coloured stones displayed in the same room.

Room 3 contains an exquisite stone libation vessel shaped like a triton shell. Carving such a vessel, using only primitive drills and abrasives, must have required exceptional skill and years of patient effort. The spirals of the outside of the shell are exactly duplicated on the inside of the vessel, and the whole surface is decorated with a scarcely visible relief of daemons making a libation.

After this masterpiece of Minoan art, the Daedalic-style figurines of later rooms, clearly influenced by Egyptian art, seem crude and mass-produced, though the last room contains a macabre surprise – the grinning skull of a long-dead Roman with a funeral wreath of gold olive leaves garlanding his cranium. The skull came from a large Roman cemetery on the edge of Ágios Nikólaos. Placed in the mouth of the deceased was a 1st-century AD silver coin; such coins were placed in the mouth to pay the ferryman who, in Roman mythology, conveyed the dead to Hades across the River Styx.

Archaeological Museum, Odós Konstantinou Paleológou 74. Tel: (28410) 24943. Reopened after renovation Tue–Sun 8.30am–3pm. Closed Mon.

Lake Voulisméni

Right in the heart of the town is another stretch of water – Lake Voulisméni, surrounded on its western and southern sides by high creeper-clad cliffs, and on its eastern and northern sides by pavement cafés and restaurants positioned to take advantage of the lake views. So deep is the lake in proportion to its circumference that it was once thought to be bottomless. In fact, it is now known to be 64m (210ft) deep at the centre, with steeply sloping sides. Small boats can pass between the lake and the sea thanks to a channel dug in 1867–71.

Alongside this channel is the town's original harbour where glass-bottomed
(*Cont. on p72*)

Tour: The Lassíthiou Plateau

The famous windmills of the Lassíthiou Plateau are highly photogenic, but increasingly rare. Even so, the plateau scenery certainly justifies a visit.

Allow at least 4 hours – all day if you plan to visit the Díktaio Andro (Díktaean Cave).

1 Aposelémis River Valley

To reach the picturesque Aposelémis River valley from Iraklíon, head east on the National Highway towards Ágios Nikólaos. After 25km (16 miles) look out for the right turn signposted to Kastélli, Tzermiádho and the Lassíthiou Plateau. This road follows the broad Aposelémis River valley through the village of Potamiés to the start of the Lassíthiou Plateau. It looms ahead like a cliff wall. Note the knob on the crest of

the ridge, known as The Nail. This outcrop was the site of a Minoan peak sanctuary where, intriguingly, the old religious rites continued to be practised for some 400 years after the final destruction of the Minoan palace culture in 1450 BC.

Go through the village of Goniés and turn right at the next junction and continue to the road signposted to Krási.

2 Krási

Occupying an elevated spot above the Mokhós Plain, Krási is worth the detour to admire the massive plane tree on the main square where tourists can be seen linking arms to see how many people it takes to encircle the trunk.

Continue along the same road for around 2km (1¼ miles) until you reach the Moní Kerá.

3 Moní Kerá

The Moní Kerá (Kerá Monastery) is largely modern but its elevated site guarantees sweeping views north to Día

The rugged landscape of the Lassíthiou Plateau attracts many tourists

Island over the Gulf of Iraklíon (Kólpos Iraklíou). It is open daily 8am–1pm and 3–7pm. Nearby is the Selí Ambélou pass, which at 900m (2,953ft) offers spectacular views of the whole Lassíthiou Plateau to the south. Rows of ruined windmills line the crest of the ridge.

Descend into the plain and at the next junction turn left.

4 Tzermiádho

Scenic Tzermiádho is the capital of the plateau villages. On its far side, a signpost points to the Trapéza (or Krónio) Cave, the site of recent excavations that can be reached by a short footpath.

From Tzermiádho centre, follow the signs to Ágios Konstantínos.

5 Ágios Konstantínos

In Ágios Konstantínos it is well worth visiting the Cretan Folk Museum. Housed in a typical Cretan cottage dating from 1800, it is open daily 10am–6pm, although often closed in winter. The village is also a popular stop for visitors to the Díktaean Cave (*see p81*).

Either continue round the plateau rim back to Iraklíon or take the more challenging route via Neápoli.

6 Neápoli

Popular with backpackers, the route back to Iraklíon via Neápoli village is rugged but scenic.

Head back towards Ágios Konstantínos and take the right turning beyond the village signposted to Neápoli and Ágios Nikólaos.

The bustling port at Ágios Nikólaos

boats and luxury motor cruisers offer trips to Spinalónga Island (*see p87*), or night-time tours of the bay with dinner and Greek dancing. Running southwest from the harbour are the town's principal shopping streets, Odós 28 Octóbriou and Odós Roussou Koundoúrou (*see p152*).

Mirabéllo Bay (Kólpos Mirampéllou)

Ágios Nikólaos sits on Mirabéllo Bay, the Bay of the Beautiful View, so-named by the Venetians who built a harbour here in the 13th century. Well protected from the prevailing westerly winds, the mirror-like surface of the bay contributes to the town's appeal, and there is a long waterfront promenade running north from the harbour along which to stroll and enjoy the views.

Ágios Nikólaos is 70km (43 miles) southeast of Iraklíon.

Eloúnta

Eloúnta village has developed into a chic resort built around a harbour where fishermen can often be seen sorting and cleaning their catch and repairing their nets. Some visitors to eastern Crete prefer this quieter resort to the bustle of Ágios Nikólaos further south. To the south of the town, signposts pointing to 'The Other Side of Eloúnda' (*sic*) direct you down a long causeway to Spinalónga peninsula, with its walks, birdlife and fine coastal views.

Magnificent views over the Gulf of Mirabéllo are also to be had from the hills surrounding the town, especially on the winding road west, signposted to Neápoli, which leads to the hilltop site of ancient Dríros. Here the remains of an *agora* (market place) and public buildings can be made out, including the footings of an 8th-century BC temple to Apollo Delphinios: though they may not look much, these remains represent one of the very first classical temples ever built in Greece, and are, therefore, of great archaeological importance.

72km (45 miles) east of Iraklíon, 12km (7 miles) north of Ágios Nikólaos.

Gourniá

Gourniá is one of the best examples of an ancient Minoan town. It sits on a low hill near the safe anchorage of Mirabéllo Bay, and the finds from the site indicate that it was a thriving industrial centre involved in pottery, metalworking and carpentry.

Most of the visible remains date to the New Palace period (1700–1450 BC), although there was a settlement here in the Old Palace period (from 1900 BC). The houses of the village were once several storeys high, and the very substantial walls that remain represent the basements, used for storage and as workshops, rather than the living areas. Turning left as you enter the site, you will walk up one of the main streets of the town, with its original paving intact. The street curves to the right and climbs to a flat area known as the Town Court. To the left (north) of this are the massive walls of a palatial building that may have been the residence of a local governor. The entrance to the palace site is marked by a flight of four steps. To the left of this is a huge stone slab, pierced by a hole in one corner. It has been suggested that this was an altar on which bulls were sacrificed; others have proposed that the slab was merely a butcher's block and that the Town Court served as a market place rather than as a ceremonial or sacrificial site.

Bearing left from the slab, walk downhill to the palace's massive sandstone east façade. Continuing down the path, ignore the first flight of stairs and take the second right that leads to a small shrine where cult objects associated with the Snake Goddess were found. From this point there is an excellent panorama of the whole site.

Gourniá is 90km (56 miles) southeast of Iraklíon, 21km (13 miles) southeast of Ágios Nikólaos. Open: Tue–Sun 8.30am–3pm. Closed Mon. Admission charge.

Ruins of streets and workshops in the ancient Minoan town of Gourniá

Ierápetra

Ierápetra stands at the southern tip of a narrow neck of land where the distance between the north and south coast is a mere 14km (9 miles). There is little of interest on the broad, flat plain to the north of Ierápetra, but wild-flower lovers should look out for the entrance to the Monastiráki Gorge on the east of the road, a great cleft in the rock renowned for its plants. In Episkopí, 5km (3 miles) further south, an unusual 12th-century church lies almost hidden, below road level, opposite the unmissable, large modern church. Excavations have revealed that the church replaced an earlier one, perhaps 4th century in date, overlying a series of catacombs, or Early Christian burial chambers.

Ierápetra itself is the southernmost town in Europe, the biggest town on the south coast and a thriving tourist resort. Thanks to an earthquake that destroyed the town in 1780, there are few signs that this was once a Mediterranean trading port, particularly under the Romans. Displays in the small Archaeological Museum (*open: Tue–Sun 8.30am–3pm*) merely hint at the richness of the ancient town; important exhibits are the Minoan clay coffin, painted with hunting scenes, and the 2nd-century AD statue of the Roman goddess Demeter.

Down on the harbour, the restored Venetian Fortress (*open: summer daily 8am–8pm; winter 8.30am–3pm*) provides a more recent parallel for the

Ierápetra's Venetian harbourside fortress

earthquakes that destroyed the island's Minoan palaces in 1700 BC. In this case, it was in 1780 that the fort collapsed as a result of a massive earthquake, killing 300 men of the garrison. Just up from the harbour, signposts point to a house in which it is claimed (on very slim evidence) that Napoleon stayed one night in 1798, during his Egyptian campaign.

From Ierápetra, it is possible to take the south coast road east to Sitía, diverting after 21km (13 miles) on the new road to Moní Kápsa. The little-visited monastery of Moní Kápsa, founded in 1471, enjoys a spectacular coastal setting to the east of Ierápetra, and was largely rebuilt in the 19th century by Yerontoyiannis, a hermit who is revered locally as a saint, and whose body is preserved in a silver reliquary in the monastery church. *Ierápetra is 107km (66 miles) southeast of Iraklíon, 36km (22 miles) south of Ágios Nikólaos.*

Kritsá
The church
The church of Panagía Kerá (Our Lady of Kerá) stands on the right-hand (northern) side of the road just before the village of Kritsá, usually unmissable because of the large number of tour buses parked alongside. This tiny domed church is one of the most rewarding sights on Crete and by far the best on the island for Byzantine wall paintings.

The church has a complex chronology that begins with the construction of the central nave and apse in the mid-13th century, not long after the Venetian occupation of Crete. The earliest paintings are those of the apse, followed by those paintings of the dome and nave. Next comes the south aisle (early 14th century), and finally the north aisle (mid-14th century). All the paintings have been restored, and are remarkable for the vividness of their colour and bold composition.

The apse The oldest paintings in the church are those of the apse. Here the *Ascension*, on the ceiling, survives only as fragments, but saints Nicholas, Chrysostom, Basil and Gregory, dressed in priestly vestments covered with crosses and holding scrolls, are depicted in fine and intricate detail around the walls; the furrowed brows of the saints,

Eastern Crete

Panagía Kerá church, covered inside with magnificent Byzantine frescoes

and their intense gaze, help convey a sense of exceptional wisdom and holiness, and suggest that these holy men are in deep contemplation of the eternal mysteries.

The dome and nave Next in date comes the dome, where four scenes from the Bible are illustrated: *Christ's Presentation in the Temple*, his *Baptism*, the *Raising of Lazarus* and his *Entry into Jerusalem on Palm Sunday*. Other scenes on the nave walls and vault include a charming *Nativity* and a gruesome *Massacre of the Innocents* on the south side. On the opposite side, the *Last Supper* shows a table set with fashionable Venetian glass. Another sign of the strong Venetian influence

is the very rare portrait, on the north wall, lower register (below St George), of St Francis of Assisi, a Western, rather than an Orthodox, saint.

The south aisle In the south aisle, an inscription names the donors of the fresco as the people of the village of Kritsá and one Antonios Lameras. The vibrant scenes depict the *Life of the Virgin* with an unusual degree of realism. In one scene, for example, Mary and Joseph sit dejected with their heads in their hands, obviously having had a row; Mary has just told Joseph of her pregnancy and Joseph has misunderstood; a helpful angel is descending from heaven to intervene and allay Joseph's concerns about

Densely packed houses crowd the hillside village of Kritsá

the Virgin's virtue. Another scene shows Joachim, dejected in the desert, fasting for 40 days in the hope that his barren wife, Anne, will conceive (note the shepherds with their stylish cocked hats). In the next scene, Joachim and Anne rush to embrace in a scene that beautifully expresses their joy at Anne's miraculous conception of a child who will prove to be the Virgin Mary.

The north aisle The frescoes here depict the Second Coming, with a vivid portrayal of the Garden of Paradise and its bird-filled trees and rivers. The first to be admitted to the garden by St Peter (bottom right) is the repentant thief who died with Christ on the cross. Seated with the Virgin and the Patriarchs are the Wise and Foolish Virgins of the Bible story, carrying candles, and with resplendent jewellery and hairstyles. More sober is the portrait of the donor on the opposite wall, with his wife and child, dressed in fine cloaks and linen caps in the style of the 14th century. Alongside, on the west wall, the Archangel Michael is blowing his trumpet to waken the dead and call them to Judgement – another angel weighs the resurrected souls in his scales. The earth is personified by a crowned female figure holding a snake that is coiled round her head – a throwback perhaps to the Minoan Snake Goddess? *Open: daily 8am–5pm (till 2pm on Sun), but sometimes closed off season. Admission charge.*

Kritsá is 80km (50 miles) east of Iraklíon, 10km (6 miles) southwest of Ágios Nikólaos.

Lató

From Kritsá (*see p75*), it is a short drive to the site of ancient Lató. On entering Kritsá, follow the one-way traffic system to the right. On a bend, after 300m (330yds), a sign points right to the archaeological site. From here, a metalled road passes 3.5km (2¼ miles) through ancient olive groves to the site car park.

The site

Lató is a relatively late foundation for Crete, dating from the Archaic period (7th century BC), after the end of mainstream Minoan culture. As always, wild flowers and splendid views add to the interest of the site. As you enter the site gate, a red arrow on the rocks points you up and to the right along a pottery-strewn track to the imposing city gate, built of massive square blocks of solidified lava. A tiny entrance, just wide enough to allow one person through, shows that no invader could enter the city from this direction without the greatest of difficulty.

The *agora* Beyond, the stepped main street leads between the walls of shops and workshops up to the *agora* (market place) – the political and cultural hub of Lató. From here, and from the theatre terrace to the right, there are almost limitless views of eastern Crete. The deep cistern

Stone benches surround the hearths where fires burnt in honour of the goddess Hestia, Lató

nearby indicates the importance of a water supply in the event of a siege.

To the left, on a higher terrace, are the remains of civic buildings where the town archives were kept, and where a perpetual flame was kept alight as a symbol of the town's continuity and as an offering to Hestia, the ancient Greek goddess of the hearth.

Site open: Tue–Sun 8.30am–3pm. Closed: Mon. Free admission.

Lató is 80km (50 miles) east of Iraklíon, 10km (6 miles) southwest of Ágios Nikólaos, and 3.5km (2¼ miles) north of Kritsá.

Moní Tóplou
The monastic complex
Moní Tóplou, or Tóplou monastery, sits on top of a bleak and windswept rocky plateau at the northeastern tip of the island, where few other people live. Tóplou is a word of Turkish origin meaning 'armed with cannon', and the monastery has been plundered and destroyed several times, hence its fortress-like appearance today. The monastery is immensely wealthy and the monks have restored much of the complex (critics say they have destroyed its character in the process), including a fine old Cretan windmill that stands just outside the monastery walls. This survives with its internal workings intact, providing a rare opportunity to see how the canvas sails turned the giant millstones within.

The gatehouse of the ancient part of the monastery leads into a delightful shady patio, paved with cobbles. Three storeys of monastic cells surround the courtyard on three sides, with a tall bell tower, rising above the gatehouse, filling the fourth side. The tiny church to the right has a pretty wheel window and four panels set into the façade. One is carved with a Virgin and Child in relief, dating perhaps to the 14th century when the church monastery was founded. Two other panels have inscriptions recording the restoration of the church after the 1612 earthquake. The fourth panel, a grey slab covered in minute script, dates from 132 BC, and records the so-called 'Arbitration of Magnesia'.

The rulers of the city of Magnesia (now in western Turkey) were called in to arbitrate in a long-standing land dispute between Ítanos and Ierápetra. The judgement (which came down in favour of Ítanos) was recorded on this slab and on a matching slab that still survives in Magnesia. Long after the dispute was forgotten, the slab was reused, first as a grave marker, then as an altar; its importance was not appreciated until a 19th-century Classics scholar, Robert Pashley, came across it when visiting this monastery in 1834.

Icons and engravings The church contains a magnificent icon, called *Lord, thou art Great* because each of the 61 tiny scenes packed into the painting illustrates a line from this Greek Orthodox prayer. The scenes sum up the whole biblical story, from Creation to the Last Judgement, with especially lively depictions of the Story of Noah, Jonah and the Whale, and the Destruction of the Cities of the Plain.

A museum to the rear of the church contains more icons, but none as riveting as this one.

Another museum across the courtyard is devoted to 19th-century engravings of Mount Athos, once made by the monks to sell as souvenirs. A tiny room to one side of the museum is devoted to the monastery's role in the Cretan struggle for independence against the Ottomans and during World War II, when the abbot was executed for assisting the Resistance. *Open: daily 8.30am–3pm. Admission charge.*

Moní Tóplou is 150km (93 miles) east of Iraklíon, 14km (9 miles) east of Sitía.

Moní Tóplou environs

From Moní Tóplou, a scenic road runs north through a bare upland landscape populated only by hardy sheep and goats. Just when you have convinced yourself that nothing could grow here except the most hardy of shrubs, you encounter beautiful groves of date palms at **Vái**. These are a distinct species of palm, known only on eastern Crete, and recorded as early as Roman times. They have given their name to the so-called Palm Beach at Vái, a lovely, but often very crowded, stretch of white sand. Just 2km (1¼ miles) to the north are the excavated ruins of the hilltop city of Ítanos, once an important harbour involved in trade with Egypt and the Near East.

Its unique palm trees draw crowds of tourists to Vái beach

Another important archaeological site is the ancient Minoan town of **Palecastro**, some 8km (5 miles) south of Vái. There is little to see here at present, but recent field surveys suggest that the town was second only in size to that at Knossós, with the potential to yield much information about life for ordinary people in Minoan Crete.

Psychró and the Díktaean Cave

The great god Zeus, destined to become the supreme deity and ruler of the heavens, was born in the Díktaean Cave at some time back in the mists of antiquity (*see p84*). Today, that cave is one of the major tourist attractions on Crete, but it is difficult to find awe and

reverence among the crowds who throng the cave.

Practicalities

The cave entrance lies above Psychró, a village almost entirely given over to the feeding of coach-borne visitors to the cave and to the sale of souvenirs. The cave entrance is a steep 15-minute climb up a well-trodden path. You can travel up on the back of a donkey, in true Cretan peasant style, if you prefer.

This is one of the few places on Crete where you are likely to encounter heavy sales technique. Hawkers pester visitors with offers of guided tours, and you may even be told that hiring a guide is compulsory: it is not, and it is entirely up to you whether you want someone to accompany you and point out the principal features of the cave.

The cave itself echoes to the anxious chatter of ill-equipped visitors frightened that they are going to slip on the damp rock of the steeply descending cave footpath, or lose their way in the gloom. The lesson of all this is to come prepared – a torch is very useful, as are non-slip shoes and a sweater against the cold of the cave interior. You can enjoy a degree of privacy by coming early in the morning or in the late afternoon, avoiding the worst of the coach tours that congregate here in the hour or so before and after lunch.

The cave

The Díktaean Cave is located in the northern flanks of the Díkte mountain range (Óros Díkti) at an altitude of 1,025m (3,363ft). The cave consists of a vast cavern, some 15m (49ft) high and 85m (279ft) deep. At the lowest section

The view from the Díktaean Cave over the Lassíthiou Plateau

there is a small pool and a number of stalagmites that divide this part of the cave into smaller chambers. Guides will tell you that the stalagmite column to the right of the pool represents Zeus's Mantle, and that it was here that the infant Zeus was fed by nymphs on wild honey and goat's milk, while the chamber to the left is the one where Zeus was born.

The same chamber is where, in 1899–1900, archaeologists found the greatest concentration of votive offerings, including bronze and clay figurines, gold brooches and bronze axes, miniature versions of the sacred Minoan *labrys*, or double-bladed axe. These offerings had been thrown into the pool or placed in crevices and cracks around the cave wall and on the stalagmites. Most corresponded to the New Palace period on Crete (1700–1450 BC), with another group of finds dating from the Iron Age (8th and 7th centuries BC), representing a revival in the use of the cave for religious ritual. Higher up in the cave, nearer to the entrance, libation tables and altars were found along with the bones of sacrificial animals.

The legend of Zeus

Like other large caves on Crete, this was regarded as a holy place. Whether or not it really is the cave referred to in ancient myth as the birthplace of Zeus is a subject still debated by scholars. Epimenides, the poet born on Crete sometime in the 6th or 7th century BC,

A sign on the Lassíthiou Plateau

at about the time when the cult of Zeus was being revived, felt inclined to disbelieve the claims of his own countrymen. Indeed, he was the poet who famously branded all Cretans as liars (*see p61*), adding that they were 'noxious beasts' and 'evil bellies'. St Paul was later to quote these same words in writing to his follower Titus, who was sent to Crete to convert the islanders to Christianity around AD 50. The reason for this disapproval was the Cretan belief that Zeus (regarded by Greeks as immortal) was dead and lay buried beneath Mount Yioúktas (*see p61*).

Cretans have a simple answer to this accusation: their Zeus is a different one from the Greek Zeus; the Cretan Zeus, worshipped as far back as Neolithic times, was a vegetation god who died and rose again annually, rather than the Greek Zeus, the immortal

sky god, who has attributes more in common with oriental and Egyptian deities.

The Díktaean Cave is 2km (1¼ miles) south of the village. Open: summer daily 8am–6.30pm; shorter hours in winter. Admission charge.

Psychró is 62km (39 miles) southeast of Iraklíon, on the southern rim of the Lassíthiou Plain.

Sitía

Sitía is the easternmost town of any significance on Crete. If you are interested in visiting this part of the island, it makes a more interesting base than Ágios Nikólaos or Ierápetra, having an easy-going but self-assured Cretan character. Tavernas are full of local people, and the food is of noticeably better quality than in the major resorts. No visitor to Sitía on a Sunday leaves without being impressed by the vitality of the evening stroll, the *voltá*, a legacy of Venetian rule, when just about everyone, old and young, priest and people, comes out to promenade along the palm-fringed seafront in their Sunday best. The town is worth a visit in August when the importance of the local raisin and sultana crop is celebrated with its Sultana Festival. This is one of the liveliest excuses for song, dance and over-consumption to be found on Crete.

The sights

Continuing along the seafront opposite the Star Hotel are Roman semicircular rock-cut fish tanks. They are not easy to spot, being below the water line at times, and were once used for storing live fish until they were needed. On the hill is the square 13th-century fortress, the only evidence of Venetian occupation. This was reduced to a shell by the Ottomans and is now partly restored to serve as an open-air theatre.

The **Folklore Museum** is in Odós Kapetán Sífi, up from the harbour, and is notable for its collection of woven rugs, bed-hangings, blankets and baskets.

The **Archaeological Museum** is to be found in the unpromising location of an industrial estate on the Ierápetra road, sandwiched between a marble mason's yard and a graveyard for rusting and broken-down tractors. The museum is, nevertheless, well laid out and labelled. The star exhibit is a wonderful ivory statue of a Minoan youth, known as the Palecastro Kouros. This has been painstakingly pieced (*Cont. on p86*)

Setting out from Sitía to catch the fish served in the town's many tavernas

Cretan myths

The birth of Zeus

The myth begins in the time of the Titans, the primeval sons of Gaia (the Earth) and Uranus (the Heavens). Kronos (Time), the youngest of the Titans, had already dethroned his own father and castrated him in order to become king. Now, he was in the habit of swallowing his own children at birth to prevent them from robbing him of his kingship. Fed up with the loss of five children, Rhea, his wife (and sister), hid deep in the Díktaean Cave on Crete to give birth to Zeus.

Kronos got to hear of the birth and demanded his usual meal, but was given a stone wrapped in swaddling clothes instead. Zeus, meanwhile, was hidden in the Ídaean Cave where he was protected by the young warrior Kourites and the goat Amalthia, who provided everything for the baby from its horn.

Minos and the Minotaur

In time, Zeus came to overthrow his father and establish his throne on Mount Olympus. One day he fell in

The infant Zeus

Theseus and Ariadne

mounted by the bull. The fruit of this bestial union was the monstrous Minotaur – half-man, half-bull – who terrorised the court of King Minos until Daidalos invented an endless labyrinth, within which the beast was ensnared.

Theseus outwits the Minotaur

The Minotaur had to be fed seven male and seven female virgins every seven years from the city of Athens. This was the penalty the Athenians had to pay for having killed Androgo, son of Minos. One year, Prince Theseus, son of the Athenian king, Aegeus, intending to slay the Minotaur, volunteered to be one of the victims. On Crete, he was assisted by Ariadne, the daughter of King Minos, who gave him a ball of wool. Attaching one end of the wool to the door of the labyrinth, Theseus was able to retrace his steps and escape once he had killed the Minotaur. Theseus then set sail for Athens, taking Ariadne with him, though he subsequently abandoned her on the island of Naxos. When Theseus arrived back in Athens he forgot to hoist a white sail to signal his safe return. His father, Aegeus, assumed that his son had been killed by the Minotaur and leapt into the sea and drowned; the sea has been called the Aegean ever since in his honour.

love with Europa, the daughter of King Aghinor, ruler of Phinicia. He appeared in the guise of a bull, carried Europa away on his back and impregnated her. Europa gave birth to King Minos, who, with the guidance of his father, Zeus, ruled Crete wisely. His happiness was, however, shattered by Pasiphae, his licentious wife. She too fell in love with a white bull (this time not a god in disguise), and asked Daidalos, artist and inventor, for help. He built her a wooden cow covered in hide. In this disguise, Pasiphae was

together from numerous scattered fragments. The fire-blackened ivory recalls the dramatic final events that took place on Crete in 1450 BC when many Minoan towns and palaces were destroyed in an inferno.

Among the other exhibits are a number of extremely rare tablets covered in the as-yet undeciphered Linear A script (*see pp56–7*). Other rarities include a carpenter's bronze saw from Zákros, a clay wine press and a clay barbecue grill. The final section of the museum contains Roman and Hellenistic material, including some fine bronze fish hooks, nails and jewellery.

Sitía is 140km (87 miles) east of Iraklíon, 70km (43 miles) east of Ágios Nikólaos. Folklore Museum. Open: Apr–Oct Mon 9.30am–2.30pm & 5–8pm, Tue–Fri 9.30am–2.30pm & 5–9pm, Sat 9.30am– 2.30pm. Closed: Sun. Admission charge. Archaeological Museum. Tel: (28430) 23917. Open: Tue–Sun 8.30am–3pm. Closed: Mon. Admission charge.

Sitía environs
Praísos
Some of the finds in the Sitía Archaeological Museum come from the Hellenistic site of Praísos. This is worth seeking out, especially in spring, when it is carpeted in wild flowers. It was a major town of the Etocretans mentioned by Homer, and the rump of the Minoan peoples who survived the conflagration of 1450 BC and who continued with the old religious practices. Defensive works can be seen, as well as one fully excavated 3rd-century BC house, with extant olive press, water cistern and mortar.
15km (9 miles) south of Sitía.

Spinalónga
The beautiful but tiny offshore island of Spinalónga makes a popular excursion from both Ágios Nikólaos and Eloúnta. In both cases, tours depart from the harbour at regular intervals during the day, and the round trip takes about four hours. There may be an opportunity to swim during the trip and refreshments are served on the larger boats – otherwise, be sure to take something to eat and drink with you.

Spinalónga peninsula
You will see Spinalónga peninsula on the right-hand side (east) of the boat if you are travelling from Eloúnta, and on the left of the boat travelling from

AYÍI PÁNTES NATURE RESERVE
If you are taking the longer trip, from Ágios Nikólaos, the boat will first pass the offshore island nature reserve of Ayíi Pántes (All Saints), where the magnificently horned Cretan wild ibex is protected from hunting. Known as the *agrími*, or more popularly as the *krí krí*, this shy beast, which features in Minoan art, is all but extinct on the mainland. Small numbers survive in the Lefká Óri (White Mountains), but the main herd, some 200 strong, can only be seen (with the aid of binoculars) on this island.

Ancient querns and kneading trough at Praísos

Ágios Nikólaos. The peninsula is known locally as 'Big Spinalónga' to distinguish it from the island, and it is attached to Crete only by a narrow sand spit. There is little to see here now of the once-thriving Hellenistic and Roman port of Oloús that stood at the southern end of the peninsula.

Spinalónga island

Spinalónga (which means 'long thorn' in Italian, a reference to its shape and pointed profile) is noted for having one of Crete's finest and best-preserved Venetian fortresses, built here in 1579 to protect the approaches to Spinalónga Bay and the Gulf of Mirabéllo. Remarkably, it remained in Venetian hands long after the rest of Crete fell to the Ottomans in 1669, following the 21-year siege of Iraklíon.

Spinalónga was only surrendered to the Ottomans in 1715, and for several decades before that it was a place of refuge for Cretan resistance fighters, and for Christians escaping forcible conversion to Islam.

After 1715, Ottoman families were settled on the island to prevent its use as a safe haven by Cretans. When the Ottoman occupation ended at the end of the 19th century, the island was abandoned. From 1903 to 1955, it was used as a colony – in effect a prison – for lepers and others suffering from contagious diseases, a cruel and unnecessary practice. The island's lepers made what kind of a life they could among the ruins of the Ottoman village, which remains a major feature of the island to this day, albeit in a state of advanced decay.

The ruins of a Minoan palace, Zákros

Zákros

Zákros is actually two villages, separated by a winding road with spectacular eastward views to the sea. Áno (Upper) Zákros is a relatively modern and prosperous agricultural town with little to delay travellers except for a few shops and tavernas. Káto (Lower) Zákros is, by contrast, a tranquil fishing village that feels as if it were at the end of the earth, sitting on its own sheltered bay, with a good shingle beach, at the eastern tip of Crete. Yet, in its Minoan heyday, this was the site of a palace as important as that at Knossós.

History The town surrounding the palace was partially excavated in 1901, but only as recently as 1962 was the palace itself discovered. The remains, which lie to the rear of the village, are being excavated with painstaking care because they have the potential to yield important information about life in Minoan times. Much of the site is waterlogged, because the sea level has risen – or rather, the island has tilted – since Minoan times, and there is the potential to find important organic remains. It also seems that the palace remains were placed under some kind of taboo following the disastrous fire that struck both here and at other palaces on Crete, in 1450 BC. While parts of the Minoan town were reoccupied, nothing was touched in the palace, and archaeologists have even found intact bowls containing olives preserved as fresh as if they had just been picked, as well as numerous fine liturgical vessels and a considerable number of undeciphered Linear A clay tablets. An ancient labyrinth has also been discovered at the site.

Trade with the East Uniquely on Crete, this palace and town were built around a harbour, the remains of which now lie below sea level. Trade goods found by the excavators indicate that this was Minoan Crete's main gateway to the Orient, the point from which Minoan traders may have sailed to Egypt and beyond. Finds from the site include copper ingots identified as coming from Cyprus, gold and jewels from the Nile Delta, and both elephant and rhinoceros ivory, possibly from Syria. In return, Cretans would have traded dyed wool, metal vases and silver-inlaid cups; we know this from tomb paintings (dated 1520–1420 BC) in Upper Egypt depicting Minoan emissaries bearing these goods as gifts, and described, in the accompanying hieroglyphs, as 'from the land of Keftiu', which was the name that the Egyptians gave to Crete.

Workshops Minoan Zákros was also an important manufacturing centre, and tools found on the site indicate that many of the rooms on the west side of the palace were used as foundries and workshops by pattern-makers, smiths, stone-workers and jewellers, potters and perfume-makers. Stores of unworked marble and steatite, a soft carvable rock-like soapstone, were also found, along with a marvellous vase, now in the Archaeological Museum in Iraklíon (*see p29*), carved from rock crystal.

The palace It seems that the immediate environs of the palace were used by craftsmen working under the control of the palace inhabitants. As for the palace itself, it has a number of unusual features, including a unique circular chamber, fed by a spring, in the living quarters to the east of the court. This was surrounded by pillars to support a roof and has eight steps leading down into it. The chamber has been interpreted both as an aquarium and as a swimming pool – if the latter, it is the very first example of a prehistoric swimming pool ever identified.

Open: daily, summer 8am–8pm; winter 8.30am–3pm. Free admission.

Zákros is 170km (106 miles) east of Iraklíon, 44km (27 miles) southeast of Sitía.

Western Crete

Western Crete consists of the two provinces (nomoi) of Réthymno and Chaniá, with populations of 90,000 and 160,000 respectively (45,000 and 55,000 in the provincial capitals). Both provinces are dominated by high mountains that rise gently from the northern coast, where most of the towns and villages are located, dropping very steeply to the narrow coastal strip on the southern side of the island.

Beaches

Beach lovers looking for the choicest spots in western Crete should consider the strip from Chaniá to Máleme, and the lonely beaches stretching south from Falásarna. The beach at Falásarna itself is famous for its soft sand and glorious sunsets. To the north, along the coast of the wild, unspoilt Gramvoúsa peninsula, there are numerous isolated beaches and sandy coves to explore, many of which are only accessible by boat. To the south, along the southwesternmost coastline of Crete, are the idyllic coral islands of Elafonísi. From here, the coastline towards the east becomes more rugged, but as you approach Chórasfakion and Fragkokástelo, the beaches become soft and sandy, lapped by shallow waters that are ideal for swimming.

Mountain peaks

In Chaniá, the peaks of the Lefká Óri (the White Mountains) fill the horizon whenever you turn your eyes to the south. They are named after the snows that cover the long east–west ridge for six months of the year (November to April) and because the grey-white limestone screes that rise above the tree-line look like snow during the summer months. This is serious mountaineering country, and those who make it to the top of Páchnes (2,453m/8,048ft) have been building a massive cairn on the summit for some years. Their objective is to erode the 3m (10ft) height difference between this, Crete's second-highest peak, and Tímios Stavrós (2,456m/8,058ft), the island's highest peak, also referred to as Mount Psiloreítis or Mount Ida, located at the western end of the Psiloreítis range in the adjacent province of Réthymno. Climbing Tímios Stavrós does not represent quite the same challenge since well-marked shepherds' tracks lead up to the chapel on the summit. Roads also penetrate a long way up the northern slope of the range to the Ídaean Cave, where Zeus

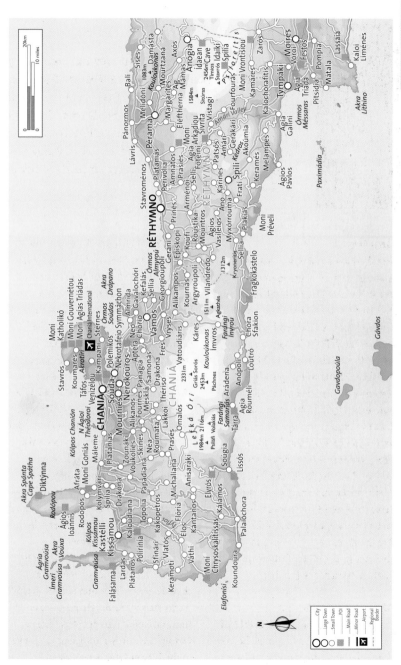

Western Crete

reputedly spent his childhood, suckled by wild goats, and where Crete's first ski centre has been established.

Natural beauty

If eastern Crete has the lion's share of the island's archaeology, western Crete wins on natural beauty. The region has numerous deep, water-eroded ravines – not just the overcrowded and popular Samariá Gorge, but also the Thériso, Ímvros and Kourtaliotiko ravines (*see p122, p102, p120, p140*), the almost undiscovered 7km (4-mile) long Agía Iríni Gorge (starting 20km/12 miles north of Soúgia), and the Arádena Gorge to the west of Chóra Sfakion. This is also the richest part of the island for botanists, with far less soil under cultivation and a great range of habitats, from beaches and cliffs to swamps and river estuaries, where wading birds and terrapins add to the biological diversity.

Provincial capitals

Above all, western Crete has the island's two most attractive towns, in Chaniá and Réthymno, the provincial capitals. Both have colourful harbours guarded by fine Venetian fortresses, and are lined with cafés and tavernas. Réthymno perhaps preserves more of its Turkish heritage, with delicate minarets of golden sandstone soaring above the domed Venetian churches, and beautifully carved wooden balconies, typical of Ottoman-style architecture, projecting from upper storeys. Chaniá, by contrast, is more of a Venetian city, its narrow streets lined with classical *palazzi* decorated with wrought-iron balconies. Here and there, a narrow gate provides a view of delightful patio gardens or shady, flower-filled courtyards, and, also like Venice, sleek cats prowl the streets as if they were the true owners.

Orange groves

Travelling west, the national highway has recently been extended beyond Kolymvári as far as Kissámou. Inland, narrow country roads weave in and out of huge citrus groves. During spring, the scent of orange blossom is

A picture-postcard view of Réthymno harbour

Breathtaking views in the Samariá Gorge

overpowering – the air is thick with the sweet smell, and equally sweet fruit that is ready for picking from late October. Green-skinned, even when ripe, Crete's oranges really are ambrosial, and one taste will make you realise why they are in such demand in the far-off markets of Athens. Away from this intensively cultivated part of the coastal plain there are some of the loneliest spots on Crete, and some of the least-visited and most unspoilt villages on the whole island.

CHANIÁ PROVINCE
Chaniá

Chaniá easily wins the title of most beautiful harbour in Crete, lined as it is with pastel-painted houses with orange-tiled roofs, varied by the strikingly exotic domes of the Mosque of the Janissaries. Enclosing the whole harbour is the 16th-century sea wall, built of cream-coloured stone, leaving open only a narrow entrance channel through which boats slip, under the watchful eye of the solidly impressive Firkás, or fortress (which now houses the Naval Museum – *see p96*).

Despite such defences, Chaniá fell to the Ottomans in 1645, the year in which the Mosque of the Janissaries was built. The Ottomans made Chaniá the capital of Crete, and so it remained until 1971 when the title passed to Iraklíon.

The legacy of Venetian rule is visible everywhere in the city, from the beautiful town houses of the old city

Stop for drinks in one of Chaniá's harbourside cafés. Gia mas!

(*see* Walk *on pp98–9*) to the massive Arsenáli, or shipyard, lining the eastern waterfront. The Ottomans built their city, known as Kastélli, on the hill above the mosque. The massive walls of their fortifications are visible from the waterfront, but bombing in World War II destroyed most of the old houses. Excavations at the heart of Kastélli (left open and visible on the left-hand side of Odós Karneváro) have revealed the tantalising remains of a massive Minoan town, whose name (preserved in Linear B clay tablets) was Kydonia.

Archaiologikó Mouseío (Archaeological Museum)

Chaniá's Archaeological Museum is housed in a large but simple 13th-century church built to serve the city's long-demolished Franciscan friary, established under Venetian rule. The exhibits provide an overview of the type of material typically found on Minoan sites in Chaniá province. There are few outstanding works of art, though cases in the north aisle contain interesting fertility figures, and there is a toy dog made from clay that was found in a child's grave.

At the eastern end of the church are several statues and mosaics of Roman date, including an appealing marble figure of Aphrodite and some highly accomplished 3rd-century mosaics from a town house in Chaniá. One contains depictions of the seasons and another shows Dionysos discovering Ariadne on the island of Naxos (*see p85*), while a third, depicting the myth of Poseidon and Amymone, is enlivened by a little vignette of fighting cockerels at the top. Off the south aisle is a little garden littered with ancient masonry whose centrepiece is a ten-sided fountain dating from the time of the Ottoman occupation.

Odós Khalídon 21. Tel: (28210) 90334. Open: summer Mon 1.30–8pm, Tue–Sun 8am–8pm; winter daily 8.30am–3pm. Admission charge.

Istorikó Mouseío (Historical Archives of Crete)

The little-visited Historical Museum is located in an elegant but faded town house in the city's early 20th-century southern suburbs. This area became fashionable from 1898 when Crete gained limited autonomy from Turkish rule, and when Prince George of Greece, appointed High Commissioner (in effect ruler of the island), chose this part of the city for his official residence. The relevance of all this becomes clear once you enter the museum, which is virtually a shrine to the heroes of the Cretan resistance and the political figures who brought about freedom from Turkish rule, and unification with Greece. Eminent Greek revolutionist Eleftherias Venizélos, for example (*see p106*), gets a whole room to himself, to the right of the entrance, and the downstairs

Chaniá's beautiful Venetian harbour, set against its mountain backdrop

corridor bristles with displays of the beautifully decorated swords and guns of Cretan freedom fighters.

At the foot of the staircase at the end of the corridor is the museum's star exhibit, a rare 16th-century cupboard carved in relief with hunting scenes. The stairs themselves feature grim reminders of World War II – a Nazi flag, an execution stake ominously hacked about at head height, and horrifying photographs of Cretan peasants and British soldiers bludgeoning German parachutists to death. Two rooms full of antique textiles and a magnificent nuptial bed are often closed but are well worth seeing when possible.

Odós Sfakion náki 20. Tel: (28210) 52606. Open: Mon–Fri 9am–1pm. Closed: Sat & Sun. Admission charge.

Naval Museum

Housed in Chaniá's Firkás, this museum explains far more than the naval history of Crete, though models of ships, from ancient Greek times until the present era, do figure prominently.

Of more general interest is the splendid scale model of Chaniá in the 17th century, complete with its monasteries, synagogue, arsenal (dockyard) and fortifications. Alongside, a beautifully drawn map shows which of these Venetian

(Cont. on p100)

Chaniá town plan (*see pp98–9 for walk route*)

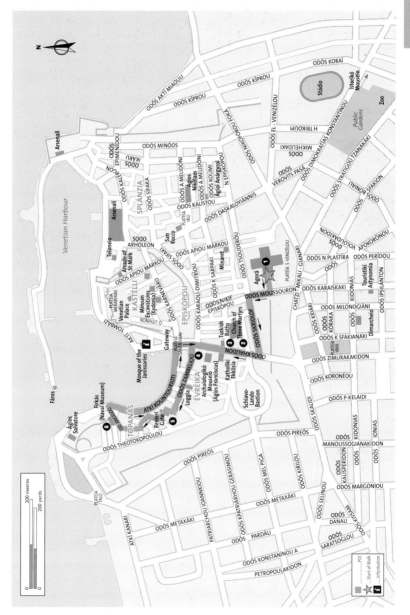

Walk: Chaniá

This walk introduces you to the intricate maze of narrow alleys in the old city and harbour area (for map of route, see p97).

Allow 1 hour – but longer if you are tempted to browse in some of Chaniá's best shops.

1 Market hall

Start at the cross-shaped market hall, an elegant neoclassical building of 1911, packed with good things to buy for picnics or presents. From the newspaper kiosk at the centre of the market, head west, past the fish stalls, and exit from the building down the café-lined flight of steps.
Turn right then first left into Odós Skridlóf.

This street is known as 'Leather Alley' for obvious reasons – bags, belts and sandals are hung from the shop awnings in such profusion that it is impossible to proceed at anything other than browsing pace. The prices here are very keen; the only problem is too much choice!
Once through Skridlóf, turn right down Odós Khalídon.

2 Church of Three Martyrs

On the right is the Church of Three Martyrs. Although it has a pleasing façade, this church is disappointingly modern within.
Continue along Odós Khalídon.

3 Turkish baths

Genuinely ancient, by contrast, are the former Turkish Baths, further down on the right, topped by 12 domes sitting like a dozen eggs in a box. Part of the bathhouse is now used as a bronze-workers' foundry.
Carry on up Odós Khalídon.

4 Archaeological Museum

On the left is the Archaeological Museum, housed in the former Franciscan church (*see p95*), with the stumpy remains of a Gothic campanile (bell tower) to the left of the façade.

Beyond the museum is the café-lined Plateía Santriváni, a lively spot at night when buskers and street traders set up their pitch.
Just before the square, turn left into Odós Zambelioú, a typical street in the old city, crammed with characterful shops and old Venetian town houses. Where the street narrows and begins to climb, look for Odós Moschón.

5 Renieri Gate

An alley on the right leads down to the Renieri Gate, with its family coat of arms and inscriptions dating the fine classical gateway to 1608. Through the gate, immediately on the left, is the late 15th-century chapel of the Renieri family, whose town house (now Sultana's restaurant) stands alongside. Ahead, at the end of Odós Moschón, there are several more elegant Venetian palaces, some now converted to upmarket hotels.

Turn right beside the medieval-style façade of the Hotel Contessa, then left up steps beside the Amphora Hotel, pausing at the top to admire the jumble of picturesque alleys that intersect at this photogenic spot. Go straight across, then right down Odós A Gampá.

Another fine Venetian palace (now the Eugenia II Hotel), with ornate stone balconies and window decoration, terminates the street.

Turn right here, down Odós Angeloú, to reach the entrance to the Naval Museum (see p96).

6 Firkás (Naval Museum)

The museum is set in the restored 16th-century Venetian fortress known as the Firkás. From the walls of the fortress (no charge for entry), there are sweeping views of the whole harbour, with its lighthouse, sea wall, arsenal and domed Mosque of the Janissaries (see p95).

To return to the market, follow the harbour back round to Plateía Santriváni, then retrace your steps up Odós Khalídon.

Walk: Chaniá

In the maze of narrow shop-lined streets of the old Venetian city

structures have survived to this day – a surprisingly large number, in fact.

For many visitors the upstairs displays on the Battle of Crete (*see pp104–5*) will probably prove the most enthralling. The story of the battle is told in detail through old photographs, newspaper reports and war relics such as a spectacular wedding dress made from parachute silk.

Aktí Kountourioti. Tel: (28210) 91875. Open: summer daily 9am–9pm; winter daily 8.30am–3pm. Admission charge.

Outside Chaniá
Akrotíri Peninsula

The Akrotíri Peninsula juts out like a clenched fist to the northeast of Chaniá, enclosing to the south the beautiful sweep of Soúda Bay, much of which is out of bounds to ordinary mortals, being the site of a large NATO naval base. The once-peaceful peninsula is now the site of Crete's second airport, and this has stimulated major development as factories and distribution warehouses are constructed to take advantage of the airport's proximity. Even so, there are some wild and unspoilt areas to the north, including Stavrós, a pretty fishing village enclosed by high cliffs, where the final scenes in *Zorba the Greek* were filmed.

Moní Agías Triádas This 17th-century monastery lies 2km (1¼ miles) north of the airport. The sleepy monastic buildings show clearly the influence of Venetian architecture in, for example,

Agías Triádas monastery

the bell tower that rises high above the entrance gate, and in the classical purity of the church façade. The church contains carved wooden choir stalls and there is a small display of vestments, icons and illuminated prayer books. *Open: daily 8.30am–3pm.*

Moní Gouvernétou and Moní Katholikó

Keen walkers, and drivers prepared to take it slowly, can follow the track from the monastery that leads, after 4km (2½ miles), to the more remote Gouvernétou monastery. This dates from the 11th century, but is essentially a 16th-century complex, restored in 1821, with many fine Venetian-inspired details. Older still are the ruins of Moní Katholikó, beautifully sited in a ravine 25 minutes' walk down the hillside. This monastery was founded early in the 11th century by St John the Hermit. Hundreds of pilgrims come here for his feast day, on 7 October, one of western Crete's most important religious festivals.

Soúda Bay Allied War Cemetery

Another worthwhile stop is the Soúda Bay Allied War Cemetery on the neck of land just north of Soúda itself. Eucalyptus trees surround this peaceful and reflective spot on three sides, leaving open the fine views to Soúda Bay, a lovely stretch of blue water framed by peaks and dotted with the aircraft carriers of the modern NATO fleet. Here are buried some 1,527 of the 2,000 Commonwealth soldiers who died in the Cretan campaign; many of

Moving memorials to the victims of war

them are anonymous and marked by a slab that simply says 'Known unto God'.

The Akrotíri peninsula lies immediately to the northeast of Chaniá.

Táfos Venizélou (The Venizélos Graves)

If you drive east out of Chaniá, following the signs for the airport, you will climb for some 4km (2½ miles) until a sign on the left points to the Venizélos Graves. It was here on this hill, in 1897, at a very tense moment in the Cretan War of Independence, that Cretan fighters raised the Greek flag in defiance of the Ottomans. The flag was almost instantly demolished by shells fired from a battleship in the harbour (*Cont. on p106*)

Tour: The Thériso Gorge

This undemanding circular route is an appetiser for more ambitious drives. If you have come to Crete mainly to laze on the beach, consider doing this particular drive, at least, to sample a Byzantine frescoed church and one of Crete's several deep ravines.

Allow 2–3 hours.

1 Ptataniani foothills

From the centre of Chaniá, follow signs for Kastélli. After 3km (2 miles), you will pass a left turn signposted Thériso. You should ignore this sign and take the next left turn at the traffic lights signposted Omalós. The drive in the foothills of Ptataniani is straightforward and scenic with acre after acre of orange groves that fill the air with a heady scent in April and May. *Continue along this road for around 14km (9 miles) to Mnimeio.*

2 Mnimeio

Quiet, pretty Mnimeio is best known for its grim war memorial, hidden in a pine grove at the village's main junction. A glass altar displays the skulls of Cretan resistance fighters shot by German firing squads.
Take the right turn signposted Alikanós/Soúgia. On entering Alikanós turn right, then almost immediately right again, following the signs for Koufós. Turn right just beyond Ágios Yeíryios church.

Pausing to let the ubiquitous sheep and goats of Crete pass to their grazing grounds

THE MESKLÁ REBELS

Mesklá was the base for a rebellion against Venetian rule in the 16th century. Rebel leader George Kandanoleon ran a rival administration, refusing to pay taxes, until he foolishly sought to make his rule legitimate by marrying his son to the daughter of a Venetian aristocrat. Kandanoleon and his supporters celebrated the marriage in typical Cretan style. When they were all stupefied with food and drink, Venetian troops rounded them all up, and either shot them on the spot, or hanged them in surrounding villages as a grim warning.

3 Ágios Cyrgiánnis

Hidden among orange groves about 1km (²/₃ mile) from Ágios Yeíryios church you will see a red and white sign pointing right for Ágios Cyrgiánnis church. This lovely 14th-century church has lost its dome, but this allows light in so that you can study the frescoes of serene saints believed to have been painted around 1430, and two reused 6th-century pillars and capitals.
Go back to Mnimeio, this time turning right for Fournés and, once in Fournés, taking the left fork marked Mesklá.

4 Mesklá

Located high in the Lefká Óri (White Mountains), Mesklá is reached by a narrow, winding mountain road. On entering the village, find the track on the left, just after the bridge, that leads up to a 14th-century church. It has well-preserved frescoes in the nave dating from 1303.
Carry on through Mesklá for a short,

but adventurous, drive of 11km (7 miles) through Zoúrva to Thériso.

5 Thériso

The birthplace of Cretan hero Eleftherias Venizélos (*see p106*), Thériso marks the start of the scenic Thériso Gorge.
Continue along the main road heading towards Chaniá.

6 Farangi Thérissiano (Thériso Gorge)

Sheer craggy cliffs tower either side of the road through the gorge that weaves along the bottom, crossing the river again and again via numerous stone bridges. After 6km (4 miles), the road passes beneath a huge cave set in the base of a cliff with house-sized boulders strewn about the valley floor. You can stop here to listen to the music of sheep bells echoing across the sides of the gorge and to enjoy the rich and varied wild flowers before continuing to the end of the gorge and back to Chaniá.

The Battle of Crete

The Battle of Crete took place in May 1941, but the events remain a talking point in the island's cafés to this very day, and carefully tended war memorials are found on the main squares of almost every village on the island. These record the names of men, women and children, priests and monks, shot in reprisal for Cretan acts of resistance during the war.

Churchill's plan

Churchill intended that Crete should be a safe haven for Allied troops driven south through Greece by the seemingly inexorable progress of German troops during the spring of 1941. He referred to Crete as an island fortress, believing that the British Mediterranean Fleet would be able to keep the Germans at bay, whilst the 32,000 British, Greek, Australian and New Zealand troops evacuated from Greece and the Balkans recouped their strength.

For a while this plan succeeded, and the Allied fleet drove off several attempts by German ships to invade the island. Frustrated, the Germans threw tens of thousands of troops into an airborne attack on Crete, which began on 20 May 1941.

Parachutists rained out of the sky over the Máleme airstrip (see p115). Many were shot before they even touched down and others were killed by Cretan villagers, armed with primitive clubs and pitchforks, as they struggled to release themselves from their parachutes. For several hours, the Allied troops beat off the attack but, at a critical moment, poor communications led to Hill 107 being evacuated, and the Germans seized the advantage. With this hill secured, it was not long before German troop planes were landing at Máleme without resistance.

The evacuation

Realising that all was lost, Allied commanders concentrated on evacuating their weary troops from Crete as fast as possible. This involved an arduous trek through the White Mountains to the southern shores of Crete where, under heavy aerial bombardment, ships took the troops off to the Egyptian port of Alexandria. It would have been a simple matter for the Germans to have halted this evacuation, if they had not been held up by a heroic regiment of Greek troops who defended a strategic river crossing for two whole days.

The aftermath

German reprisals against the Cretan population for the troops lost in the invasion only served to increase resistance. Local people kept up relentless guerrilla warfare against the invaders – at a heavy cost in terms of human life – for the entire duration of the war.

The beautifully tended Allied cemetery at Souda Bay

below, one of which also hit the church. The ship that fired the shells was itself sunk the next day, an act of divine revenge, according to devout Cretans.

Among the partisans who raised the Greek flag on that day was Eleftherias Venizélos (1864–1936), a prominent figure in the War of Independence, who went on to become prime minister of Greece in 1910. He survived one assassination attempt and, in 1935, having led an abortive republican coup, was condemned to death by victorious monarchists. He avoided execution by fleeing to Paris where he died shortly after. To Cretans he remains a hero and an almost saintly figure. He is buried on this beautiful and restful hilltop site high above Chaniá, together with his son, Sophoklés.

If for no other reason, the panoramic views make this spot worth seeking out – additional attractions include a pleasant tree-shaded park (good for a lunchtime picnic) and the little Byzantine church of Profitis Ilías that stands close to the graves.

Chóra Sfakion

Off-season Chóra Sfakion is a quiet, unspoilt fishing village on the south coast that makes the ideal base for a hideaway holiday if all you want to do is walk, swim and enjoy good food in waterside tavernas. However, from May to October, it is also the bustling transit point for swarms of hungry hikers coming off ferries from Agía Rouméli, the exit of the Samariá Gorge, to take buses back to Chaniá. The ferry service also links Chóra Sfakion with Soúgia, Palaióchora and Gávdos island (*see pp117–20*). The timetable changes regularly, so be sure to check when and where the boat actually calls!
75km (47 miles) southeast of Chaniá.

Once a sleepy fishing village, Chóra Sfakion now has a choice of hotels

The ruins of Fragkokástelo Castle have inspired tales of ghosts!

East of Chóra Sfakion Here the countryside is flat and intensively cultivated, with a rash of villa developments and one of the prettiest villages along this coastline. The village of Fragkokástelo is famous for its role in Crete's history. Dating back to the Bronze Age, Fragkokástelo is said to have been an important Christian settlement in the early Byzantine period. Remains of what are believed to have been extensive basilicas, the 6th-century-built Ágios Nikitás and Ágios Astratiós, survive to this day.

Standing in the foothills of the Lefká Óri (White Mountains), Fragkokástelo is dominated by the splendid 14th-century fortress, the Fragkokástelo Castle. It was built ostensibly to protect the southern coast against piratical raids but, in fact, the castle was more often used for quelling the local population. Nearly 400 men lost their lives in this peaceful spot in 1828 when Cretan insurrectionists, led by Khátzi Mikhális Daliánis, were massacred by an overwhelming force of Turkish soldiers. Local people say that a ghostly army, known as the *drossoulítes* (literally meaning 'dew shades'), returns at dawn to dance on the plain in front of the castle every year on 17 May, the anniversary of the massacre.

Despite a grim history the castle is tailor-made for children, as well as adults, to explore. It was built in 1371 to the designs favoured by the Venetians when constructing fortresses, and although extensively renovated in the 19th century it is said to look almost exactly as it did 640 years ago.

It has four square towers with mighty walls topped by battlements. Its main entrance is decorated with a series of coats of arms carved into the walls, which are said to be those of important families who lived in the area. Inside, there are the remains of buildings that would probably once have been used for cooking, as stables, and for storage of grains and arsenal.

The castle stands right beside a fine and sandy beach, washed by warm and shallow waters that make it ideal for families. If you love to snorkel, then make the short walk along the beach to where sand gives way to rock formations that reach the sea. A little inland is the monastery of Ágios Charalambós where you can see a particularly elaborate wooden iconostasis in its church and a series of monks' cells. With its history and tales

of ghostly happenings, Fragkokástelo is a village on many a tourist's tour. Many stay, and there are apartments available to rent, some overlooking the sea.

West of Chóra Sfakion Only one road goes west of Chóra Sfakion, a twisting, steep and narrow road that drops vertiginously away to the south and is not recommended to nervous drivers. This passes, just to the west of the town, a group of beachside caves. One of these is named the Cave of Daskaloyiánnis in honour of the 18th-century rebel who led the Cretan struggle against Turkish rule and reputedly used the cave as a hideout. Daskaloyiánnis came from Anópoli, the next village along the road, once a rebel stronghold, now renowned for its carpets of spring wild flowers. Here there is a choice of routes: on foot to Loutró, or by car, along a newly made road, to Arádena. The delightful village of Loutró, about two hours' walk due south along a steep downhill footpath, is the site of an ancient harbour, to which St Paul was heading when his boat was blown off course. (He was eventually shipwrecked off Malta.) It sits on a very beautiful bay, with the added attraction that the only way in and out is by boat or on foot – though this has not deterred recent villa development.

Arádena, by contrast, is a near-deserted village and a delight to explore. It sits on a stony arid plateau, backed by the Lefká Órí (White

Wild flowers abound in and around the spectacular Arádena Gorge

The quiet beach at little-visited Falásarna

Mountains) whose peaks rise sheer behind. Like several other isolated and abandoned villages on Crete, the former inhabitants migrated to other parts of the island – or even overseas – in order to make a better living. Some have returned and are starting to restore the decayed buildings, and one wealthy family has donated the new iron bridge that provides access to the village across the spectacular Arádena Gorge. Hand-painted signs in the village point down deserted cobbled streets to the white-domed church of Mikhaíl Archángelos, with its 14th-century frescoes, just visible through the door-grille if the church is locked. To the right of the church is the old road, a broad pebbled path that was the only way into and out of the village

until the new bridge was built. The path leads to the edge of the ravine and then plunges down into it, following a zigzag path up the other side. If you follow this path (well worth doing for views and the wild flowers), allow about an hour to reach the top on the other side.

Kastélli

Kastélli (sometimes known as Kastélli Kissámou) is a bustling and prosperous town serving the local agricultural community. Here you are likely to come across furniture-makers at work outside their workshops, cobblers making Cretan riding boots, and old-fashioned bakers using wood-fired ovens. The museum in the main square has long been closed for restoration. If it ever reopens it is worth visiting for its fine collection of Roman statuary, including finds from Diktýnna, the 2nd-century AD temple that sits at the tip of the Rodopós peninsula, to the east of Kastélli. A rough track leads across the peninsula to the temple site but it is not recommended for cars. Instead, it is better to hire a boat from nearby Kolymvári (*see p111*).
Kastélli is 43km (27 miles) west of Chaniá.

Kastélli environs

Falásarna The ancient port city of Falásarna lies to the west of Kastélli, and is well worth visiting both for its ruins and for the huge and little-visited

Western Crete's Elafonísi (*see pp112–13*) is famous for its pink sand

sandy beach. Approaching Falásarna from Plátanos, there are fine views down onto the beach and across the Gramvoúsa peninsula. The port ruins are some 1.5km (1 mile) from the Falásarna Hotel, near the end of a rough track. Passing masses of polythene tunnels, you know you have nearly reached the site when you pass a large and prominent stone 'throne' on the left (its real purpose is not known). The site is littered with equally huge blocks of tufa that have tumbled from the ancient city's collapsed walls over the years.

The entrance is located next to a prominent circular tower, also part of the city's 3rd-century BC defences, alongside of which is a square cistern with its original plaster-and-pitch lining intact. From here, you descend to the flat harbour basin, once under water but now left high and dry by tectonic movements that have lifted this western end of Crete by about 9m (30ft).

Square trenches in the base of the harbour have been left open by archaeologists, at the bottom of which you can see massive masonry blocks jumbled up with pebbles. The theory is that the harbour, built in the 4th century BC, had virtually fallen out of use by the 1st century BC but, being enclosed and hidden, was used by pirates as a base for attacking Roman ships. Once the Romans had conquered Crete, they therefore deliberately and permanently blocked the harbour entrance with these huge stones.

If you have the energy, you can climb the hill to the northwest of the harbour, passing little Ágios Gíorgios church, to reach the hilltop acropolis, with its fine views. Alternatively, you can simply enjoy swimming from the nearby beach and exploring the many rock pools.

Polirinía Some 7km (4 miles) south of Kastélli is the ancient city of Polirinía, a rare example of the kind of city that developed in the post-Minoan era. Cretan society ceased to be highly centralised, and scores, if not hundreds, of small communities were set up, each controlling their own territory. It was probably the lack of water that resulted in Polirinía's abandonment, though the inhabitants did not move far – only down to the base of the hill to the site of today's village, where springs are

abundant. From this village, several paths lead uphill to the church (usually locked), built on the site of a Hellenistic-era temple and incorporating Roman masonry into its external walls. From the church, a broad path leads through flower-filled olive groves to the massive walls that surrounded the ancient city. Higher still are the jumbled ruins of fortifications built when the site was briefly reoccupied in the 10th to 13th centuries. Winding through the walls are goat tracks that eventually lead to the crest of the hill, from where there are fine views over the Gulf of Kíssamos (Kólpos Kissámou).

Kolymvári

Much of the coastline west of Chaniá has been developed for tourism, and only when you get as far as Kolymvári
(*Cont. on p114*)

The picturesque village of Kolymvári has so far escaped development

Tour: The Elafonísi islands

Livas, the hot south wind, creates the largest waves of the Mediterranean Sea in the Elafonísi islands, which lie at the southwestern edge of Crete. These unspoilt islands and beaches are difficult to reach and this drive once involved covering long distances on winding roads.

Allow 4 hours for the drive.

1 Falásarna

From Kastélli Kissámou, take the westward road to Plátanos, and then the right turn signposted to Falásarna (*see pp109–11*). Here you can visit the fascinating ruins of the town's 4th-century BC port.

Continue through the village, heading towards Sfinári.

2 Sfinári

On approach to Sfinári you will see scenic hills with the sea always in view.

Greenhouses pepper the fertile plain below. Growing bananas and out-of-season salad vegetables for export to the Greek mainland is a major industry around Sfinári.

Head out of the village on the road signposted to Kámpos.

3 Kámpos

Break in picturesque Kámpos, before continuing to Keramotí and Kefáli. From this road, enjoy sweeping views right over Stómio Bay (Ormos Stómiou).

Keramotí village

At Kefáli, turn right immediately after driving through the village, following the sign to the Moní Chrysoskalítissas.

4 Moní Chrysoskalítissas

Meaning Golden Stair, the Moní Chrysoskalítissas is a beautiful white-walled convent with powder-blue roofs. Leading down to a cove are 90 steps, of which one is said to be made of gold (*khrisos*), but only those who are free from sin are able to see it! There has been a hermitage here since at least the 13th century.

Take the new road from Moní Chrysoskalítissas to Elafonísi.

5 Elafonísi

Despite the many buses and coach tours that head for the coast, busy Elafonísi and its islands are still Crete's most stunning beaches. Pink-tinged shell-covered sands are complemented by warm clear waters and rock pools full of fish. The sea is shallow enough for you to wade across to the nearest island and find another lovely beach.

Return along the road to Kefáli, turning right to pick up the road to Élos.

6 Élos

The capital of the region, Élos is known as the Kastanochória, meaning the Chestnut Village, because of the sweet chestnuts grown here as a commercial crop. In July, the air is thick with the scent of blossom, while in late October, the village celebrates its harvest with a festival.

Continue along the main road to Koutsomatádos.

7 Topólia Gorge

Shortly after Koutsomatádos, the dense woodland either side of the road gives way to the spectacular cliffs and caves of the Topólia Gorge. The scenery is breathtaking.

Continue to Kaloudiana.

8 Kaloudiana

After the excitement of the gorge, the road descends rapidly to the scenic village of Kaloudiana.

From here, turn left to return to Kastélli Kissámou or right to join the Chaniá highway at Koléni.

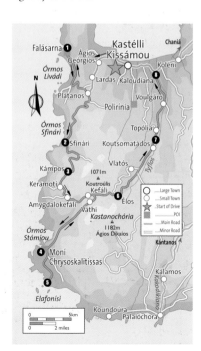

Tour: The Elafonísi islands

Moní Goniás is situated right by the sea

do you return to the real Crete. Local people come here for the renowned seafood restaurants, but few tourists follow in their wake. Those who do will find an attractive and self-confident town with a pebble beach, numerous rock pools and crystal-clear waters teeming with small fish.

Ágios Ioánnis Church An even less accessible site on the peninsula is the church of Ágios Ioánnis (St John), reached by means of a very rough track (the walk takes two to three hours) from Rodopós. This is the route taken by thousands of pilgrims every year on 29 August (the feast of the birth of St John the Baptist), when boys sharing the name John (Ioánnis) are brought from all over the island for mass baptism. For the rest of the year this lonely shrine is deserted.

The Diktýnna Boat operators offer trips from Kolymvári out to the northeastern tip of the Rodopós peninsula, site of the Diktýnna, one of the ancient world's most famous temples. The Diktýnna, or Diktiynnaion, thrived from Hellenistic times (the 3rd century BC) through to the Roman era. The goddess Díktynna was, like Diana, a huntress, usually depicted with her dogs, protectress of the mountains and countryside. She was worshipped all over the Greek, and subsequently the Roman, world, with temples to her honour in Marseille, Athens and Sparta. This was her chief sanctuary and it has been suggested that Díktynna represents the survival of a deity from Minoan times – she may have derived from the mountain mother goddess worshipped in Minoan peak sanctuaries. This temple was visible from far out at sea, but the remains, excavated in 1942 by occupying German troops, now consist of little more than a massive paved terrace on which her shrine once stood. The lack of visible structures does not deter visitors from coming here, however, because the sheltered cove below the sanctuary site is excellent for swimming.

Goniás Monastery Much closer to Kolymvári is the lovely Moní Goniás, which dates mainly from its rebuilding in 1662, though it incorporates masonry of several periods. An early 17th-century stone balcony to the right of the gatehouse is supported on brackets carved with ferocious Venetian lions. Opposite the gatehouse is a Turkish fountain (1708), whose Greek inscription reads: 'O flowing spring, pour water for me; water is vital to life, the sweetest element'. Through the gatehouse is the graceful monastic church containing fine examples of woodcarving, such as the abbot's chair.

Best of all are the outstanding 17th-century icons: those on the iconostasis of the central nave are the work of a Cretan monk called Parthenios. An icon in the north aisle (dated 1637 and signed by Konsantinou Paleokaia, also known as Palaiókapas) shows

German war graves at Máleme

St Nicholas in bishop's robes seated on a scarlet cushion. Adjacent is an earlier work, the mid-15th-century figure of Christ as High Priest. The serene Virgin and Child in the south aisle is of the mid-17th-century period.

To the east of the church is a shady terrace with views to the distant hills of the Akrotíri peninsula. Embedded in the rear wall of the church is a cannonball from the Turkish bombardment of 1866, when the monastery came under attack for its role in the rebellion against Turkish rule. To the left of the church is a small museum with an outstanding icon, *The Crucifixion* (1637) by Palaiókapas.

Goniás Monastery is 1km (²/3 mile) north of Kolymvári. Open: daily 8.30am–3pm.

Máleme

The German invasion of Crete began at Máleme on 20 May 1941 (*see pp104–5*), and today it is the site of the German War Cemetery. The cemetery stands on Hill 107 where much of the fighting took place and where many of the German paratroopers who took part in the airborne invasion were picked off with bullets as they floated to the ground. The statistics of the battle make grim reading and are a sober reminder that more than three times as many Germans died in the campaign as did Commonwealth troops (6,580 German troops killed or missing, compared with 2,000 on the

The indigenous *Cyclamen creticum*

Máleme environs

Ágios Stéphanos From Spiliá, drive on south through Drakóna, then, after 1.5km (1 mile), look for a white sign pointing right to Ágios Stéphanos church. This 10th-century building lies at the end of an oak-shaded path renowned for the white cyclamen that flower on the left-hand bank in spring (these cyclamen – *Cyclamen creticum* – are similar to *Cyclamen repandum* found on mainland Greece).

The walls of the ancient church are cracked and subsiding, but the 13th-century frescoes remain clear enough for a Nativity scene to be made out, and, below it, the Stoning of St Stephen, the first Christian martyr, while next to both is a Pentecostal scene. Evangelists are painted round the tiny apse, but the scenes on the south wall are far more difficult to interpret.

Mikhaíl Archángelos Just 1km (⅔ mile) further south a big sign points right to the extraordinary church of Mikhaíl Archángelos, known as the Rotonda because of its unusual central dome. From the outside this consists of

Commonwealth side). The small pavilion at the entrance to the cemetery, with its map showing the progress of the battle, does not record how many Cretans suffered in this war – for it was they who bore the brunt of the awful reprisals taken by the Germans once the island was in their hands.

Today Hill 107 is a peaceful spot; the lower part is managed to encourage wild flowers in spring, and the upper part is packed with neat graves that spread all the way up to the hill crest. Here a terrace offers views over Máleme airstrip, the focus of the German assault and still in military use today. *Máleme is 16km (10 miles) west of Chaniá.*

CYCLAMEN

Cyclamen creticum, found nowhere else in the world other than Crete, favours the island's shady gorges and scrubby woodland. Considerably smaller and less showy than its cultivated relatives, its delicate white flowers and leaves appear between March and May, with the plant surviving and spreading underground by tubers outside this period.

a stepped series of concentric rings, diminishing in size as they climb upwards. Inside, the church resembles a beehive, with the side walls pierced by six tall arches, one of which frames the apse. On the floor there are the remains of 6th-century mosaics with a geometric pattern, while frescoes of standing saints cover several walls.

The church is unique in its plan and shape, and archaeological excavations are in progress in and around the church, aimed at discovering more about its history. These suggest that the church is a rare survivor of the so-called First Byzantine period (mid-5th to mid-6th century), but with frescoes from the 10th and 12th centuries.

Spilía The countryside south of Máleme is dotted with small village churches that are far older than a first glance would suggest. Three in particular are worth a visit. Spilía is reached by heading west to the Kolymvári crossroads, then south for 3km (2 miles). Drive on through the village of Spilía until you see a blue signpost pointing right to the church at the village exit. You first pass a little square on the right, shaded with plane trees and with a little gabled fountain in one corner. The church is another 500m (550yds) on from the square, on a grassy mound to the right of a sharp bend. The simple building dates from the 12th century and the soot-blackened frescoes inside from the 14th century. They depict scenes from the life of the Virgin, including a lively Nativity with the Three Kings on the south wall, and the Presentation of Jesus in the Temple on the opposite wall.

Palaióchora
From being a small southern-coast fishing village, Palaióchora has recently expanded to become one of the island's
(*Cont. on p120*)

Palaióchora's Venetian castle walls rise above the ferry harbour

Tour: The Ímvros Gorge

If you are not up to walking the Samariá Gorge, there are several possible substitutes, including this lazy way of enjoying the Ímvros Gorge by car.

Allow at least half a day.

1 Vrýses

Coming from either Chaniá or Réthymno, take the well-signposted turning off the National Highway to Vrýses (*see pp125–6*). This attractive town is the meeting point of five roads and is a popular stopping-off point for hungry travellers.

Follow signposts to Chóra Sfakion and then after 5km (3 miles) turn left, signposted to Alíkampos.

2 Alíkampos

The road to Alíkampos runs through the foothills of the Lefká Óri (White Mountains). After less than 1km (²/₃ mile), look for a concrete embankment on a right-turning bend, and turn left down a road to the church of the Panagía. Numerous springs gush out of the hillside and are channelled into a 16th-century Venetian cistern (restored 1909). A grassy downhill road to the left

The road follows the cliff tops above the gorge

leads to the church, idyllically set in an orange grove. The frescoes (dated 1315) are some of the best preserved in Crete and depict biblical scenes, from Adam and Eve to the Nativity and Crucifixion. *Go back to the main road and turn left, heading towards Krapis.*

3 Krapis

As you approach Krapis the landscape is barren and rocky, but some 5km (3 miles) further on it dramatically transforms into a neat patchwork of tiny fields with a cone-shaped hill crowned by a circular Turkish fortress. *Continue on to Ímvros.*

4 Ímvros

Ímvros village marks the beginning of the gorge. You see little of its stern majesty unless you pull over at one of the numerous viewpoints along the route. The road winds round the top of the cliffs high above the western edge of the gorge. You can, however, descend into the gorge on foot from Ímvros village, following the well-signposted footpath (allow three hours to walk the whole route, and either check the times of return buses before you set out, or arrange for a taxi to collect you). *Continue on to Chóra Sfakion.*

5 Chóra Sfakion

The road now descends via a series of hairpin bends. An attractive fishing village where you can enjoy lunch in a seaside taverna, Chóra Sfakion is popular with visitors.

From Chóra Sfakion, turn right heading east to Fragkokástelo.

6 Fragkokástelo

Reached along a broad, flat coast road, Fragkokástelo (*see p107*) has a child-friendly beach of golden sand and an almost intact 14th-century castle. *From Fragkokástelo, retrace your route heading west to Anópoli, passing Chóra Sfakion.*

7 Anópoli

For a completely different experience, head west out of Chóra Sfakion on the vertiginous road to Anópoli, turning left at the taverna on the road to Arádiana. Abandoned years ago and left to crumble, the village and surrounding fields give a real sense of village life as it was before the age of concrete and plastic.

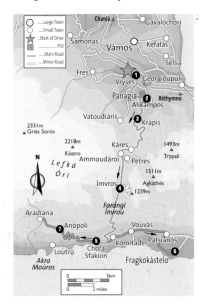

most enjoyable upmarket resorts. Several new – but small – hotels have been built, and new restaurants have sprung up along with them, although without spoiling the Cretan character. That Cretan character extends to the fact that the town centre is virtually sealed off to traffic at night, when local people leave their houses to play backgammon and drink *raki* outside the local tavernas, their chairs and tables filling the narrow streets.

Palaióchora has two big beaches that can both be viewed from the castle that sits high above the town, built in 1279 by the Venetians and consisting now of little but the encircling walls. To the left (east) of the town, is the ferry harbour and then a huge sweep of mixed sand and shingle beach. To the right (west), is a huge beach of golden sand – flying its European Blue Flag (awarded to beaches that meet the highest standards of cleanliness) with pride. The waters on this side can be cold because of the mountain streams that pour into the bay to the west. In the height of summer, this is welcome, but earlier in the year, it deters all but the very hardiest of swimmers.

Offshore breezes make this a good spot for windsurfing too, and there is a hut at the far northwestern end of the beach where boards are available for hire.

South coast ferries If you want a break from baking in the sun all day, you can take the south coast ferry from Palaióchora's harbour and head along the coast, or across the sea to the island of Gávdos. Tickets and timetables are available from travel agents in the town, or from the ferry company kiosk on the harbour.

The ferries operate between the beginning of April and the end of October. During this period there are daily services to the Elafonísi islands, to the west of Palaióchora (*see pp112–13*), and eastwards to Soúgia (*see p122*) and Ayía Rouméli (for the Samariá Gorge). Services operate five times a week in summer from Palaióchora, three times a week from Chóra Sfakíon. Off-season the service is limited.
For information, tel: (28230) 41393.

Palaióchora is 84km (52 miles) southwest of Chaniá.

Palaióchora environs
Gávdos Gávdos island is worth a trip if you want to say that you have stood on the most southerly point in Europe. The island is about two hours south of Crete by ferry, and the day trip allows you four hours to explore the tiny harbour at Karabé or walk inland to the main village of Kastrí (where there is precious little to see). Most of the islanders are farmers eking a living from the sun-bleached soil. The landscape is flat and unremarkable, but there are some fine beaches and the turquoise waters are delightful for bathing. Local people have taken to

Avoid the crowds by setting out along the Samariá Gorge at the crack of dawn

meeting the ferry and providing transport to the island's best beaches, which lie to the north and to the southernmost tip of the island (and of Europe), Tripití point.

Soúgia Remotely located at the end of a long, twisting road from Chaniá, Soúgia is gradually being discovered by tourists for its pebbly beach, translucent waters and simple fish tavernas lining the shore. Across the sea lies the distant island of Gávdos, while across the beach, to the east, you can make out the remains of the ancient Roman port of Elyrós either side of a small river estuary. To the west of the village, a well-marked path (very steep in places) makes for the ruins of a 4th-century BC temple to Asklepios (god of healing) at Lissós, some 3km (2 miles) across the cliffs.

Samaria Gorge (Farángi Samariás)
After Knossós, the Samaria Gorge is the best-known attraction on Crete, and every summer tens of thousands of people trudge the 15km (9-mile) long path that follows the bottom of the gorge, finding none of the tranquillity and solitude that one normally associates with walking in the countryside. If you hate crowds, set out early in the day (the gorge opens at 6am) or walk one of Crete's other, equally spectacular, ravines.

The gorge is only open from the beginning of May to the end of October because flash floods are a very real danger in the rainy season.

There is no road access to the southern end, so your only way back is by ferry (to Chóra Sfakion, Soúgia or Palaióchora), or by retracing your steps up the gorge (there are rooms to rent in Agía Rouméli, at the southern end of the gorge, so it is perfectly feasible to do this over two days).

The times of ferries and connecting buses can be checked at one of Crete's tourist information centres (the times vary according to the season). Of course, you can leave the logistics of getting to and from the gorge to somebody else by signing up for a coach excursion, though this means setting out with a crowd of 30 or more people. You can also hire a taxi to get you there and arrange to be collected at Agía Rouméli. One or two taxis are available for hire in Agía Rouméli itself, and they will take you back to Chaniá or anywhere else on the island – provided you get to them before someone else does. If all else fails, there are plenty of rooms for rent in Soúgia, Palaióchora and Chóra Sfakion, where you can spend the night.

In the gorge The total length of the gorge is 13km (8 miles), and it is another 2km (1¼ miles) to the coastal village of Agía Rouméli with kilometre posts marking out the route. You should allow at least five hours to do the walk. Keep your entrance ticket as

Georgioúpoli is one of several upmarket resorts on the Vámos peninsula

you will be asked to hand it in at the exit – this is a simple device to help the park wardens count the number of people in the gorge, and send in the rescue services, if necessary, to locate stranded walkers. You should take sufficient food and drink to sustain you along the route (there are tavernas at either end, but not within the gorge itself). Drinking water is supplied from taps at six points along the gorge, four of which also have toilets.

The lazy way If you do not feel like tackling the whole gorge, there are two alternatives. One is to walk the first 2km (1¼ miles) or so from the northern end of the gorge; this is exhilarating, because the route plunges some 900m (2,953ft) down the so-called Xylóskalo ('Wooden Staircase'), through beautiful pine woods; the obvious drawback is that you have to climb all the way back up, and 900m of staircase is no joke.

The other option, known as 'The Lazy Route', is to tackle the gorge from the southern end. Despite the name, this involves a stiff uphill climb to the gorge entrance (2km/1¼ miles), followed by a walk of about 4km (2½ miles) through the narrowest part of the gorge, where the path is squeezed between towering cliffs, up to 600m (1,969ft) high. You can go all the way up to the gorge's most famous landmark, the so-called Iron Gates (Sidherespórtes), where the sides of the gorge close in to leave a gap of a mere 3m (10ft). To get here involves a there-and-back walk of about 11km

(7 miles), so you might just as well walk the whole gorge.

The Samaria Gorge begins 43km (27 miles) south of Chaniá, on the Omalós Plateau, and runs southwards to end 2km (1¼ miles) north of Agía Rouméli. Admission charge, and boat fare to Chóra Sfakion.

The Vámos Peninsula ✕
The Vámos Peninsula east of Chaniá has recently been 'discovered' by upmarket tour operators, so that its coastal villages – Kalýves, Almrída and Georgioúpoli – are developing a rash of new villa complexes around their margins. For the present, they remain largely unspoilt, and make an excellent base from which to explore western Crete by car.

Beaches and wild flowers Kalýves and Almrída, both on the western edge of the Vámos peninsula, have sandy, gently shelving beaches, perfectly safe for children to play on. Beyond here, a network of narrow lanes threads the peninsula, well worth exploring for the wild flowers.

The northern and eastern edges of the peninsula are stony and exposed to wind, so hundreds of tiny fields have been created by clearing the soil and using the rock to form drystone walls. Stone-paved paths thread their way between the walls, and some fields, no longer cultivated, have been recolonised by masses of flowers.

THE LEGEND OF ÁPTERA

The name Áptera means 'wingless'. According to legend, this was the site of a competition between the muses and sirens to see who sang better. When the sirens lost, they were so mortified they threw off their wings, which caused them to fall into the sea and drown. Their beautiful white wings were transformed into small islands – identified as the Lefke Islands in the Soúda Bay.

If your explorations take you through the village of Gavalochóri, stop to look at the little museum, reached up the lane opposite the war memorial. This contains miscellaneous objects collected by the villagers, from old photographs to weapons from World War II.

Áptera After the detour to Samonás, the road through Stílos passes a turning, just before Megála Khoráfia, that leads to the ruined hilltop city of Áptera. The extent of the overgrown ruins indicates just how large this post-Minoan city was. Its exact foundation date is not known, but it was flourishing in the 7th century BC and was occupied until the Arab conquest of Crete in AD 824. The walls can be traced for a circuit of some 4km (2½ miles), but the most obvious remains are those of the Ottoman-era fortress, standing at the highest point on the hill, and offering extensive views over the Vámos peninsula and Soúda Bay. Also visible is a Venetian fort on a prominent hill to the north – this is now used as a prison.

Georgioúpoli Georgioúpoli is named after Prince George, son of the king of Greece, who was appointed High Commissioner of Crete from 1898 to 1906, ruling the island in the interim period when Crete still technically belonged to the Ottoman Empire but enjoyed a measure of autonomy. The prince used to enjoy coming here for the hunting, and the area is still renowned for its birdlife. The Almirós River flows into the sea at this point, and the marshy margins of the river are a haven for birds, as well as for freshwater crabs, terrapins, frogs and fish. Locally the Almirós is known as the 'Turtle River', and you can hire pedal boats or take boat trips at the village's fishing harbour for exploring its reed-fringed banks.

Georgioúpoli also sits on the western edge of a huge and often deserted sandy beach that spreads for 12km (7 miles) in the direction of Réthymno. Although affected by the *meltemia* (northern summer winds), the beach is popular in places and has plenty of space.

Vrýses and Samonás Another attractive feature of Georgioúpoli is the wonderful green avenue of giant eucalyptus trees that forms the old road out of the village (once the main road, but now superseded by the National Highway). Following this will bring you to pretty Vrýses, famous for its creamy yoghurt and wild honey, and on to Néo Chorió. Here it is well worth diverting to Samonás for Crete's most appealingly sited church, Ágios Nikólaos. If you want to go inside the church, call at the house of the guardian, which is on the left at the village exit. The guardian or his wife will come with you and open up the church.

Just beyond the village you will catch your first glimpse of the church, beautifully sited on a knoll in a lovely green valley, with no other building in sight. Built of attractive honey-coloured stone, with a tall central dome, the church dates from the 11th century, and the frescoes inside, including a tender Virgin and Child, were made sometime between 1230 and 1236.

Georgioúpoli lies 33km (21 miles) east of Chaniá and 26km (16 miles) west of Réthymno.

RÉTHYMNO PROVINCE
Réthymno

Réthymno is a very likeable city from which vehicles have largely been excluded, leaving the narrow streets to the bustling hubbub of human traffic. Watching the parade of people up and down the main street is an enthralling pastime, especially from the comfort of one of the numerous pavement cafés clustering round the Rimóndi Fountain. The shopping is excellent (if more expensive than Chaniá) and the town remains

Réthymno's café-lined Venetian Harbour is the centre of the city's bustling nightlife

Réthymno town plan (*see pp128–9 for walk route*)

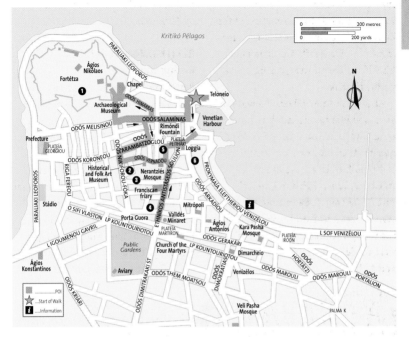

essentially Cretan, with traditional boot-makers, and ironmongers selling axes and sickles, mixed in among the tourist shops selling embroidery, lace and T-shirts.

Another feature of the city is its architecture, a legacy of Venetian and Ottoman rule. Look up in almost any street and you are sure to see ornamental balconies and elaborate window frames above the modern shopfronts. Look down alleys and you will see doorways carved with coats of arms, cherubs, vines or crouching lions, or crumbling façades propped up by timber buttresses waiting to be restored.

Archaeological Museum

Réthymno's Archaeological Museum is housed within one of the defensive bastions opposite the main gate of the Venetian Fortress (*see p131*). Light floods into the museum from its central atrium, around which are top-quality displays of sculpture, coins, pottery and jewellery from excavations in Réthymno province.

The museum provides an excellent introduction to all the various crafts practised by the Minoans. Here you will find beautiful and delicate pottery that would not look out of place on a modern dinner table. From various caves

(*Cont. on p130*)

Walk: Réthymno

Réthymno, with its narrow traffic-free streets, tempting shop displays and traditional architecture, is tailor-made for strolling. To make the most of this walk, come at dusk, when the sunset views from the Fortétza are stunning (for map of route, see p127).

Allow 1 hour.

Start at the Customs House end of the Venetian Harbour where the fishermen gather to mend their nets. There is a small fish market here most mornings, opposite Benetsianíko's bar, and there is also a good view of the 16th-century Venetian lighthouse.

Turning your back to the harbour, take the road to the left, then second right (Odós Salamínas), then second right (Odós Himárras).

1 Fortétza

This road leads up to the Fortétza, passing first the Centre of Contemporary Art, which hosts temporary exhibitions of modern Greek art. The whole area around the museum is developing as a centre for young artisans, and you can see jewellers, icon painters and potters at work as you stroll. The road ends at the entrance to the **Archaeological Museum**, on the right (*see p127*), and the Fortétza on the left (*see pp131–2*).

Coming out of the Fortétza, head straight down the steep cobbled ramp that leads to Odós Melisinoú, turn left, and then second right (Odós Xanthoúdidou) beside the Fortezza Hotel.

By night, this narrow street and all the others in the vicinity are packed with taverna tables. Take the third right (Odós Arambatzoglóu), and follow it to the little square at the top. Turn left here (Odós Nikiforoú-Fóka), then first left into Odós Vernadóu.

2 Historical and Folk Art Museum

This street has many fine houses in the Venetian architectural style, including the grand palazzo, halfway down on the right, which is now the home of the Historical and Folk Art Museum.

Continue down Odós Vernadóu.

3 Nerantziés Mosque

A short distance further down is the elegant Odeion concert hall, better known as the Nerantziés Mosque. Originally built as a church in the mid-16th century, it was converted to a mosque in 1657 and given its stylish minaret in 1890. Today the building is used as a music school (closed to the public).

At the end of Odós Vernadóu, turn right into the city's crowded main street, Odós Ethníkos Antístáseos. Walk up the street to explore the fascinating range of shops and the market at the far end, up against the 16th-century Porta Guora, all that remains of the Venetian city walls. Coming back down the street, take the third left (Odós Áyios Fragkískou).

4 Franciscan friary

Take a look at the fine gateway of the 16th-century Franciscan friary, now a school.

Continue on Odós Ethníkos Antístáseos past the mosque and take the first right on to Plateía Petiháki.

5 Rimóndi Fountain

Cafés dominate this end of the street and cluster thickly around the Rimóndi Fountain. Built in 1629, it has three lions' heads spouting water into a beautiful marble basin.

6 Loggia

To the right of the fountain, Odós Paleológou contains the 16th-century Loggia, used as a meeting place for the Venetian nobility. This handsome arcaded building has been restored and is now a gallery selling good-quality reproductions of classical art.

From here, it is a short step down Odós Nearhoú back to the harbour.

Réthymno's 16th-century Venetian lighthouse

An elegant minaret, a legacy of Ottoman rule, points skyward from Réthymno's close-packed town centre

and peak sanctuaries in the province there are clay figures of priestesses and bulls. There is also a large display of clay *larnakes* (burial chests) painted with abstract renderings of sea creatures such as octopus, fish and nautilus shells. Others depict lively hunting scenes, suggesting that the Minoan countryside was teeming with wildlife.

The dead were placed in these *larnakes*, trussed up tight in the foetal position, knees to chin, and the chests were then placed in chambered tombs. Some *larnakes* have a hole in the base, which has led some archaeologists to suggest that they may originally have been used as domestic bathtubs. Such an explanation seems a touch far-fetched, as do the tortuous attempts of Minoan archaeologists to

prove that the sacred double axe symbol – the *labrys* – bears a geometrical relationship to the form of the labyrinth, the maze-like pattern that appears on coinage of the period from the 6th century BC. Examples of both coins and axes are displayed here.

Finally, there is an unusually good display of Graeco-Roman statuary, including a very fine bronze helmeted youth (probably Mercury) salvaged from a Roman ship wrecked off Agía Galíni on the south coast.

Opposite the main entrance to the Venetian Fortress. Tel: (28310) 54668. Open: Tue–Sun 8.30am–3pm. Closed: Mon. Admission charge.

Historical and Folk Art Museum Now housed in a fine 17th-century Venetian

mansion close to the Nerantziés Mosque, this is a charming collection of traditional Cretan crafts: embroidery, lace, basketware, farming tools, costumes and pottery.
Odós Vernadóu 28–30.
Tel: (28310) 23398. Open: Mon–Sat 10am–2.30pm. Closed: Sun.
Admission charge.

Venetian Fortress (also known as the Fortétza) Réthymno's massive fortress dominates distant views of the town and seems big enough to accommodate the whole population of Réthymno in times of trouble. It is said to be the biggest Venetian fortress ever built and the impressive walls encompass churches, an open-air theatre, and a whole network of underground magazines and cisterns, as well as ruined accommodation blocks for garrison troops. A climb through the pine-planted interior is worthwhile just for the views, especially at sunset. Alternatively, you can watch day turn to night from the Sunset taverna, which sits on the coastal road, below the west-facing fortress walls.

The marvellous views emphasise the strategic value of this particular headland, and its fortress was built in 1573, specifically as a base from which to stamp out piracy. In this it succeeded, but the fortress did not prove much of a defence when the Ottomans arrived in 1645, seizing the city after a siege of only 23 days – a trifle compared with Iraklíon's 21-year stand-off. The Ottomans built the big

Beneath the walls of the Fortétza

VENETIAN RULE

The Venetians changed the face of Réthymno and the whole of Crete during the 465 years of their rule (1204–1669). Venice acquired the island by questionable means (as part of the spoils of the Fourth Crusade) but compensated by building harbours, shipyards, fortresses, palaces and public buildings. At first, Venetian rule was exploitative; timber was stripped from the hillsides, heavy taxes were imposed and Catholicism was forced on the Cretan people, whipping up resentment among the Orthodox clergy. In time, however, a more fruitful relationship evolved, with Cretans and Venetians intermarrying and sending their children to Italy to be educated. As a result, the arts flourished in the 16th and 17th centuries, the period known as the Cretan Renaissance. This was the era that produced Mikhaíl Damaskinós, the great icon painter (*see p36*), and the even more famous El Greco (*see p34*).

domed mosque, the most prominent building in the interior.
Odós Salaminos. Tel: (28310) 28101. Open: summer daily 8am–7pm; winter daily 8.30am–3pm. Admission charge.

Outside Réthymno
Anógia

Anógia is well placed to serve as a base for exploring the villages and sights that lie along the northern flank of the Psiloreítis mountain range. Part of Anógia's appeal lies in its reputation as a weaving centre; tour buses bring people here to watch weavers at work and to shop for blankets, wall hangings, and shoulder bags of brightly coloured woven wool. The town has a traditional air, but most of the buildings date from

the post-war era: Anógia was destroyed in August 1944 for being, in the words of the German commander on Crete, 'a centre of British espionage and an asylum for resistance bands'.
Anógia is 45km (28 miles) southeast of Réthymno.

Anógia environs

Fódele Fódele is promoted as the birthplace of the artist El Greco (born Doménikos Theotokópoulos), who, it is said, was born here in 1541. In fact, it is more likely that he was born in Iraklíon, but this does not stop the village exploiting the El Greco association. His family's house, which has been identified and restored to pristine newness, is signposted from the village and delightfully located in an orange grove about 1km (⅔ mile) from the village centre. Opposite is the lovely domed Byzantine church of the Panagía (the Virgin), built in the early 14th century but incorporating the nave of its 8th-century predecessor. The frescoes (dated 1323) are far from complete but have been well restored and depict saints, angels and scenes from the Life of Christ.
Fódele is 27km (17 miles) west of Iraklíon (see map p25); 50km (32 miles) east of Réthymno.

Ideon Andron (The Ídaean Cave)

South of Anógia, a steep and winding road heads south into the mountains to Crete's only ski centre, and on to the Ídaean Cave. Some claim that this cave was the true birthplace of Zeus (*see p84*), rather than the Díktaean Cave (*see p80*), which lies further to the east. Others say that Zeus was born in the Díktaean Cave but brought up in this cave. Certainly, the cave has long been revered, and is mentioned in the writings of both Plato and Pythagoras. Archaeologists are working to find out more.

If you venture up here in summer, when excavation work is in progress, you can watch the painstaking work of sifting the cave deposits. Another reason for coming here is for the wild flowers: at this high altitude (1,500m/4,921ft and above), spring comes up to eight weeks later than on the coast, so you can see a mass of bulbs and other wild flowers as late as June. The high pastures also support seasonal grazing, and the shepherds still use the traditional circular stone huts that dot the landscape as places of shelter, and as dairies, where the animals are milked and the milk is made into cheese.

Tílisos From Fódele, a new road leads north to join the Old Highway, now superseded by the New Highway running along the north coast. From here, the best way to Anógia is via Tílisos, a town that, remarkably, preserves something like its ancient (*Cont. on p137*)

The Ídaean Cave where, according to mythology, Zeus spent his infancy

Tour: The Amári Valley

The Amári Valley is rich in Byzantine churches, providing an excuse to explore an area full of spring wild flowers and little visited by other tourists. The churches are often closed but the key can usually be tracked down quite easily – ask at the nearest kafeníon. Take a torch for illuminating the frescoes.

Allow at least half a day.

1 Amári Valley

From Réthymno, follow the Old Road east along the seafront until you come to Perivólia, then turn right signposted Amári. Pass under the National Highway and continue through this scenic route at the start of the broad Amári Valley, looking out for the turning on the right to Chromonastíri.

Take the road on the left signposted Ágios Efíchios just before you reach Chromonastiri.

2 Ágios Efíchios

About 2km (1¼ miles) along this country road the domed church of Ágios Efíchios comes into view. Its frescoes, which date back to the 12th century, are among the earliest to survive on Crete.

Back on the Amári road, continue to Ágía Foteiní, turning right at the village junction to Méronas.

3 Church of the Panagía

Surrounded by the lush countryside of the Amári Valley is the Church of the Panagía in the village of Méronas. It has frescoes dating from 1339. The delicate icon of the Virgin is late 14th century and one of the oldest on the island.

Head back to Ágía Foteiní and turn left just after the village exit to Thrónos.

4 Thrónos

The tiny church in the centre of Thrónos has a Venetian-influenced Gothic portal, along with a collection of 14th-century frescoes. Remains of a geometric mosaic run to the excavated footings of its 4th-century predecessor. Further down the street, a concrete path on the left (signposted Sybrítos) leads uphill to the recently excavated site of the ancient Amári Valley capital.

Return to the main road and after about 2km (1¼ miles), just past the turning to Kalóyeros, park on the right.

5 Agía Paraskeví

From this vantage point, you get the most spectacular view of the valley and the domed church of Agía Paraskeví. Here lies the grave of Yeóryios Khortátzis, a 15th-century local clan leader. A decayed fresco depicts him in armour on horseback taking leave of his wife to fight against the Venetians.

Continue along the road about 3km (2 miles) to the crossroads.

6 Moní Asomáton

The Asomáton monastery, a magnificent walled and fortified structure now used as an agricultural college, stands at the crossroads. Although private, nobody usually objects if you go in the courtyard to look at the 13th-century church whose furnishings are now in the Historical Museum of Crete in Iraklíon (*see p33*).

Turn right in front of the monastery and drive to Amári.

7 Amári

The modern capital of the region is best known for its church, the Agía Anna, along the road opposite the police station. The damaged frescoes in the apse contain an inscription dating them to 1225, making them the oldest firmly dated frescoes on Crete.

Return to the centre of Amári and continue along the main road to Tympáki.

8 Tympáki

The road from Amári to Tympáki offers fabulous scenery. From the town, you can reach the cluster of archaeological sites around Festós (*see pp42–5 & pp62–3*) before returning to Réthymno.

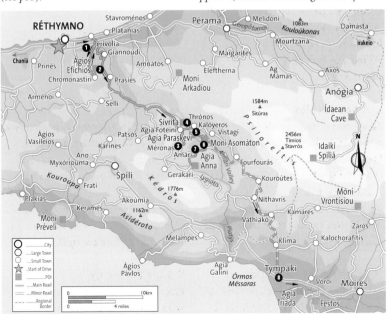

Moní Arkadíou church, with its Baroque façade, has become a symbol of Cretan heroism

Minoan name – it is called Turiso in Linear B clay tablets. It is also the site of three large Minoan villas dating from the New Palace period (1700–1450 BC). These have survived remarkably intact – in the case of Villa C, the walls stand almost to first-floor level, with flights of stone stairs leading up to what would have been the living quarters. The villas have features similar to the great palace sites, such as lustral basins (for washing and anointing visitors), shrines, treasuries and rooms full of giant storage jars. There are also rooms in Villas A and C with drains leading through the outer walls: these have been interpreted as possible toilets.

Tílisos is 10km (6 miles) west of Iráklion (see map p25). Villas open: Tue–Sun 8.30am–3pm. Closed: Mon. Admission charge.

Moní Arkadíou (Arkadi Monastery)

A symbol of Cretan heroism in the cause of independence and a literal expression of the Cretan battle cry – 'Freedom or Death' – Moní Arkadíou has now been designated a European Memorial of Freedom. It was here that hundreds of resistance fighters blew themselves up rather than surrender to the Ottomans during the 1866–9 revolt. Huge numbers of people converge on the monastery every 9 November to commemorate the mass suicide.

The siege and its aftermath The siege began on 7 November 1866, when Ottoman soldiers surrounded

the monastery. Hundreds of Cretan guerrillas had sought refuge inside, along with their wives and children. The Ottomans eventually demolished the now-rebuilt gatehouse, and poured into the deserted monastery courtyard.

Abbot Gabriel instructed the Cretan defenders to withdraw to the now-roofless gunpowder store, which is at the far left-hand side of the courtyard. He waited until the last minute before giving the word to light the powder kegs, so as to trap and kill as many Ottomans as possible in the explosion. The abbot was killed by the Ottomans, and a rebel called Kostis Giamboudakis blew up the kegs.

Nearly 300 rebels were killed, as were 600 women and children, along with 1,500 Ottomans. Only 3 Greeks escaped, and another 100 were taken into captivity and tortured.

The event stirred complacent politicians into action all around Europe. Until then, powerful countries – Britain, France and Italy included – had stood by idly and ignored the atrocities being committed by the Ottomans in Crete. It took another 30 years for Crete to gain a semblance of self-determination.

Museum memorial In the centre of the courtyard is the church with its fine Baroque façade (dated 1587). To the right, the museum is full of mementos of the siege: Turkish swords and cannon, portraits of some of those who

(Cont. on p142)

Priests and monks

If your idea of a typical priest or monk is that of a humble, pious and charitable person, think again when it comes to Crete. Monks, especially, and many priests regard themselves as the aristocrats of the island and it is not unusual for them to treat those they consider their inferiors with a degree of arrogance that is quite untypical of Crete as a whole.

Focus of learning and resistance

Cretans know the score and pretend a head-bowing deference to any monk that crosses their path. This exaggerated respect, afforded even by the most cynical of atheists, can be attributed to the key role played by the Greek Orthodox Church during the dark years of the Turkish occupation, and again during the German occupation when the Church served as the focal point for Cretan resistance. Priests and monks also ran clandestine schools under Turkish rule, in defiance of the ban on Christian education and worship, keeping alive the flame of

A priest taking a break from his duties

Monks and priests are a highly visible and integral part of life on Crete

Greek nationalism. Great acts of heroism were committed by the predecessors of today's monks and priests. The major powers ignored the plight of Crete under the Ottomans until the rebels of Arkadíou monastery (*see p137*) committed mass suicide in 1866. This event drew attention to Turkish brutality, galvanising Europe into belated action. Again, during World War II, the monks at Préveli Monastery (*see p143*) suffered vicious reprisals because of the help they gave to Allied troops escaping the island by submarine to Egypt.

Waning influence

For all this, memories of the past are beginning to fade and the influence of the Church in the everyday life of the Cretan people is on the wane, at least in the urban centres. Even so, monks (who remain chaste) and priests (who are allowed to marry) maintain a highly visible presence in Cretan society, with their uncut locks and beards and their black cassocks, and no Cretan would consider an event in the life of the community complete – whether a school prize-giving or a wine festival – without the blessing and official presence of the clergy.

Tour: The Kourtaliotiko Ravine

This short but rewarding drive will take you through a ravine, reminiscent of the famous Samaria Gorge, to Moní Préveli, the monastery overlooking the sea. Take respectable clothes for admission to the monastery but plan to leave them off if you visit the nearby beaches.

Allow at least half a day.

1 Cemetery of Arménoi

Take the road south out of Réthymno, past the public gardens, signposted to Spíli. After 8km (5 miles) turn right at the signpost to the Late Minoan Cemetery of Arménoi (*open 8am–3pm daily except Mon*). Here the rock-cut tombs date to the late second millennium BC. The site is covered in orchids and anemones in spring.

Back on the main road continue for 12km (7 miles) and take the right turn signposted to Plakiás/Préveli Monastery.

2 Farángi Kourtaliotiko (Kourtaliotiko Ravine)

Heading along the road you turn a corner and the ravine opens out in front of you. Part way down on the left is a layby. Pull in here to experience the

Crossing the ravine

clattering breeze that gives the ravine its name ('Windy Gorge').

At the southern end of the short ravine, enter Asómatos, then turn left signposted Moní Préveli and left again.

3 Moní Préveli

About 2km (1¼ miles) on is a spot where walkers dip their feet in the Megapótamos (literally 'Big River'), just before the ruins of the original 16th-century monastery, Moní Préveli. Its successor, built in the 17th century, lies 4km (2½ miles) further along the winding road, on a cliff-top terrace with sea views (*for the monastery and its museum, see pp143–5*).

Driving back to the bridge, look out for the left turn signposted Plakiás and then the left turn to Lefkógia.

4 Lefkógia

Lefkógia is a quiet village and beyond it tracks lead left down to a series of pretty coves backed by caves.

Turn left out of the village for Plakiás.

5 Plakiás

Plakiás sits in a lovely sheltered bay with sweeping views. It has glorious, uncrowded beaches and plenty of places to enjoy a meal and a drink.

Take the road that brought you in to Plakiás and turn left after 1km (²/₃ mile) signposted Myrthios.

6 Myrthios

Pretty Myrthios, clinging to the mountains overlooking the sea, is one of several hamlets you pass returning to Réthymno.

At the next junction, continue straight.

7 Kotsifoú Gorge

This stretch of road takes you through the spectacular, steep-sided Kotsifoú Gorge (Farángi Kotsifoú).

At the next junction, go straight on.

8 Ágios Ioánnis

From Ágios Ioánnis onwards, the road passes through delightful countryside where cypress trees shade pastures cut by streams. Just after Ágios Vasíleios, turn left to rejoin the main Réthymno road.

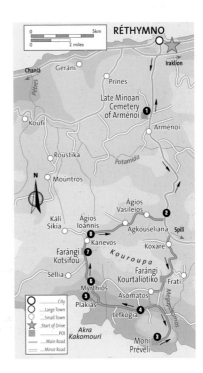

died, the vestments of Abbot Gabriel and, most poignant of all, the shrapnel-scarred and hand-painted banner of the Cretans who died in the defence of the monastery.

Moní Arkadíou is 26km (16 miles) *southeast of Réthymno. Museum open: daily 8.30am–3pm.*

Moní Arkadíou environs
Eléftherna Eléftherna is the site of a fascinating post-Minoan hilltop town.

The seemingly isolated Préveli monastery has often been at the centre of momentous events

Just beyond the village entrance sign, a concrete track leads downhill to the right, signposted 'To Ancientry' (*sic*). This leads to a Roman villa built of materials salvaged from ancient Eléftherna – the sheer quantity of richly carved marble indicates the wealth of that city.

Heading back up the idyllic gorge, you will pass a fine 10th-century church beside a spring. Back in the village turn right and follow signs to the Acropolis Taverna. Parking by the taverna, you can follow the track to the right that leads to the ancient hilltop city, poised on a ridge between two deep gorges.

The most prominent of the ruins is a late Roman tower; note how the rock-cut path in front of it has been carved into a grid to resemble paving. Another rock-cut path goes to the left of the tower and after some 300m (330yds) runs out – turn left here and, immediately on the left, you will find a series of huge rock-cut cisterns, of cathedral-like proportions, cut into the cliffs below the city, and supported by a forest of pillars.

Eléftherna is 65km (40 miles) to the east of Réthymno by road (10km/6 miles of footpaths surround Eléftherna).

Moní Préveli (Préveli Monastery)

Moní Préveli enjoys an idyllic setting on the steep hills that sweep down to the sea on the south of the island. One 19th-century traveller described the setting as a Cretan paradise, and 'one of the most happily chosen spots for a retreat from the cares and responsibilities of life'. In fact, Moní Préveli has seen more than its share of tumultuous events and is another of those monasteries that have played a conspicuous role in Cretan history.

Centre of resistance The monastery was founded in the 16th century, on a site that lies further inland: the ruins of the original monastery still stand, alongside the Megapótamos River, on the road up to the present-day monastery. It was moved to this more secluded position after the Ottomans took Crete. The new monastery, with its precious library, became a clandestine centre of learning under the Turkish occupation, and successive abbots took a leading role in organising local revolts against the Ottomans.

From 1866 on, following the explosion that killed the rebels at Moní Arkadíou (*see p137*), British sympathisers with the Cretan cause raised funds to buy a ship – the *Arkhadi*. This made regular trips to Crete, through the Turkish blockade, carrying weapons and supplies for the Cretan rebels, which were landed at the beach just to the east of this spot; again it was the monks of Moní Préveli who organised their distribution.

The Battle of Crete Moní Préveli also played a key role in sheltering

The Megapótamos River joins the sea at Moní Préveli

Commonwealth troops during the evacuation that took place at the end of the Battle of Crete in May 1941 (*see pp104–5*). The same beach below the monastery was used by the submarines that took troops off the island to the Egyptian port of Alexandria. A plaque in the monastery courtyard records the fact that hundreds of British, Australian and New Zealand soldiers were protected by the monks and guided to the beachhead from where they made their escape: all this 'in defiance of the ferocious reprisals suffered by the monks'.

The monastery today Among the reprisals taken by the Germans was the partial destruction of the monastic complex. The monks themselves, however, had already destroyed what ancient building fabric and frescoes had remained from the 17th century in their own rebuilding works in 1835. The buildings today are therefore relatively recent, but they make a harmonious ensemble.

The church contains a splendidly carved and gilded iconostasis, covered in scenes from the Life of Christ. Some of these date from the mid-18th century, and have been transferred here from churches in the Préveli region to protect them from theft. The monastic museum is housed in the former stables where rock-cut mangers are now used as display cabinets. Exhibits include liturgical silver, and the vestments (dated 1701–10) of Abbot Jacob Préveli, the monastery's founder.

Monastery open: daily 8.30am–3pm. Admission charge.

Palm Beach The little beach, which has so often featured in the history of Moní Préveli and Crete, lies to the east of the monastery, and can be reached from the monastic complex along a marked path. Allow at least half an hour and be prepared for some scrambling over steep and rocky terrain. If the beach is not too crowded, this can be a lovely spot.

The Megapótamos River flows into the sea at this point, and its banks are lined by groves of beautiful palm trees, the same rare Cretan native palms that grow at Vái (*see p79*). The whole estuary resembles a desert oasis, backed by the harsh rocks of the Kourtaliotiko Ravine.

From the beach, you can continue eastwards, along rough tracks, for another 3km (2 miles) to the church of Agía Fotinis, one of numerous little churches lining this part of the southern coast. Agía Fotinis dates from the late 14th century, and its walls feature frescoes of the female saints Fotiní, Marína, Paraskeví, Kyriakí and Eiríni.

Moní Préveli is 38km (24 miles) south of Réthymno (see pp140–41 for a suggested driving route).

Getting away from it all

Until the 1970s, Crete had almost no roads; a situation, in Cretan eyes, brought about by their Ottoman rulers who deliberately suppressed the island's economy and made no investment in infrastructure. Instead, the island was covered in a network of tracks connecting one village with the next, along which goods were transported by donkey.

Supplementing these medieval roads were footpaths, called *kalderími*, paved with local stone and usually sheltered from the sun by high walls. Where they survive these paths nearly always link one church to the next, or a village to its fields, and their walls support a wide variety of plant life.

WALKING ON CRETE

For the tourist, this web of paths provides a great opportunity to explore the island on foot. It is also the best way to admire the rich and varied flora.

Unfortunately, seeking out the vestiges of this medieval network is increasingly difficult. The *kalderími* are slowly becoming choked with scrub from lack of use, and tracks are progressively being concreted over or tarmacked for the benefit of motorists.

Guides and equipment

The presence of tarmac very much depends upon the wealth of the local community: inevitably, it is the poorer inland regions where tracks survive and where the walking is best. As these are remote regions where help is a long way off, basic precautions are essential. Do not set out without telling someone (such as your hotel) where you are going and when you expect to return. Take plenty of water, high-energy food supplies and protection against the sun. The best practical guides to exploring Crete on foot are two pocket books published by Sunflower Books called *Landscapes of Eastern Crete* and *Landscapes of Western Crete* (for maps, see p183).

Guided tours

If you want someone else to handle the logistics of your walk, join one of the guided tours offered by **The Happy Walker**, *Odós Tobazi 56, Réthymno (tel: (28310) 52920)*. This organisation offers a different walk each day of around four hours' duration, led by a knowledgeable English-speaking guide.

When and where to go

Spring (from April to mid-May), when the weather is pleasant but relatively cool, is by far the best time to go walking on Crete.

Autumn (mid-September to October) also brings fine walking weather, but the countryside will be scorched by the summer heat, lacking spring's abundance of colour. The Samaria Gorge is Crete's most famous walk (*see pp122–4*), but as a result of its popularity the path is crowded and noisy: for a quieter and equally magnificent route, consider walking the Ímvros Gorge instead (*see pp120–1*).

The south coast offers some excellent walking, using Loutró or Chóra Sfakion as a base (*see p106*). For more experienced climbers, the Lefká Óri (White Mountains) present a serious challenge. The **Kallergi mountain refuge** (*tel: (28210) 33199*), open from May to October, is run by the Greek Mountaineering Club of Chaniá (EOS) (*tel: (28210) 44647*), and is used by climbers as a base for crossing the range via Páchnes (2,453m/8,048ft), Crete's second-highest peak. Reaching the summit of Crete's highest mountain, Tímios Stavrós (a mere 3m/10ft higher at 2,456m/8,058ft), is relatively easy for fit and well-equipped climbers by means of a path that leads up from the taverna (closed) to the Ídaean Cave (*see pp132–3*).

Head to the coast for wonderful walks

THE FLOWERS OF CRETE

Visiting Crete in the summer, it is difficult to imagine just how colourful and rich in wild flowers this stony landscape can be in the spring. Geography and geology combine here to provide myriad ecological niches. The climate varies significantly from the coastal zone, via the temperate uplands to the alpine slopes of the central mountains. Within these divisions, the range of soil types adds to the potential for diversity, and a marked feature of Crete is the abundance of plants that are found in one site only, and nowhere else on the island.

When to go

The true wild-flower enthusiast will find plants of interest throughout the year. The Cretan spring really begins as far back as October, when heavy rains bring the first crocus and narcissi, and when new grass and freshly germinated seedlings turn the earth green almost overnight. For sheer quantity of colour,

Nature has given Crete colours in abundance

however, mid-April to mid-May is the main flowering season; the slopes of the Lefká Óri range turn from white to red as the snows melt and the scarlet anemones flower.

Where to look

Almost every roadside offers a botanical feast in spring, but for rarer plants – especially orchids – you need to head away from the intensively cultivated coastal plains (where herbicides have, sadly, denuded the fields of their native flora) to the inland and upland regions. Almost any archaeological site will provide rich hunting ground for rare species because (with the notable exceptions of Knossós and Festós) these sites are neither ploughed nor sprayed.

What to look for

Rough uncultivated hillsides abound with vivid lime-green flowers and the thrusting 1m- (3ft-) high spikes of white asphodel. In unsprayed orchards and vineyards, purple oxalis competes with scarlet anemones. Easily mistaken for anemones, but with a lovely powdery sheen and a bell-shaped flower, is the Asiatic buttercup, *Ranunculus asiaticus*, often found on field edges and embankments. *Clematis cirrhosa*, with tiny yellow bellflowers, spotted inside, scrambles all over field walls, as do many pretty bindweeds. The white-flowered Cretan cyclamen blooms in shaded woodland and on damp banks. Irises, crocus, narcissi, lilies and alliums are all relatively common, while tulips and plum-coloured fritillaries are rare. Purple and yellow orchids are easy to spot in grassland and on uncultivated slopes – though green-, brown- and white-flowered species take some finding.

Wild-flower sites

The following sites are especially rich in wild flowers. Remember not to disturb the plants in any way, but leave them for future visitors and generations to enjoy.

Eastern Crete

Gortýs (*pp45–7*) is renowned for flowers that seem to grow more luxuriously than elsewhere in this part of the island. Less visited are the flower-covered ruins of the Minoan village of Vasiliki on the western side of the road south from the national highway to Ierápetra.

Western Crete

Two easily visited sites with abundant wild flowers are the German war cemetery at Máleme (*pp115–16*) and the ancient Minoan cemetery at Arménoi (*p140*). For a longer trip, Polirinía (7km/4½ miles due south of Kastélli) is a marvellous spot for plant hunting. There is an excellent taverna in the modern village, right next to the beginning of the path that climbs up to the ancient hilltop city, or you can picnic in the ancient olive groves that surround the ruins. Meaning 'rich in lambs',

Polirinía was founded in the post-Palatial era (after 1100 BC) and flourished until the Venetian era (13th century), and its substantial remains shelter many kinds of bulbs and orchids.

The Vámos Peninsula, especially around Litsárda and Selia, has tiny fields surrounded by drystone walls crawling with rock plants. These fields, where no longer cultivated, have been colonised by sheets of sky-blue lupins. Anópoli and Arádiana, both accessible by road from Chóra Sfakion (*see p106*), combine an abundance of flowers, growing among cherry orchards and olive groves, with extensive coastal views.

Western Crete is a flower lover's paradise

Excursion to Santoríni Island

With its dazzling white houses, a skyline dotted with church domes the colour of the sea, sleepy harbours, bustling towns, vineyards and amazing rock formations, Santoríni has long been one of the most visited destinations in the Greek island group, the Cyclades. It is also one of the most southerly islands in the archipelago and, lying around 112km (70 miles) north of Crete, makes a great excursion during your stay.

You can reach Santoríni from Iraklíon. **Hellenic Seaways** (*www.hellenicseaways.gr*) and **Sea Jets** (*www.seajets.gr*) operate a fleet of vessels that run most days during the summer and take around two hours. If you fancy a more leisurely crossing, hop on board one of the daily ferries operated by **GA Ferries** (*www.ferries.gr/gaferries*). They take a little over four hours. Ferries operated by **Lane Lines** (*www.ferries.gr/lane*) also run out of Ágios Nikólaos and Sitia too, or you can take a short flight with **Sky Express** (*www.skyexpress.gr*) and make the journey from Iraklíon to Santoríni in around 30 minutes.

After a hearty breakfast, head for the harbourside at Iraklíon and look out for signs to Théra (Santoríni). You'll find the times of ferries and catamarans can vary depending on the season and weather conditions so be sure to check the day before so you can arrive in good time. Most crossings begin between 9am and 10am. Once aboard, take time to admire Iraklíon harbour behind you as you head past the island of Día for the open Sea of Crete. Your first thrilling glimpse of the Cyclades – Santoríni and the unspoilt island of Anáfi lying just to its east – will come into view ahead.

As you approach Santoríni you'll see it has an unusual crescent shape. A colossal volcanic eruption occurred here more than 3,500 years ago, which, literally, blasted away the centre of this once circular island to create a massive crater, known as a caldera. On approach you'll sail over the caldera. Ahead is the hugely picturesque Théra harbour.

Théra is the capital of Santoríni and characterised by cobbled lanes lined with tightly packed white houses and churches that appear to cling to the hillside rising sharply from the sea. This harbour buzzes with activity. Here you can watch fishermen unload their catches and dine on their fresh fish while looking out over the caldera in any one of a dozen or more restaurants. Be sure to explore Théra. Worth a look is its **Archaeological Museum** full of ancient Cycladic artifacts (*open Tue–Sun, 8.30am–3pm*).

Santoríni is not a large island and you can easily explore it on a short excursion. The best option is to hire a car or taxi. Before you leave Théra, however, be sure to check the times of your return sailing to Crete. Santoríni is dominated by mountains and a craggy coastline indented with lively black-sand beaches to the south, which are well worth exploring, while to the north of Théra is Oía, a village best known for its traditional skaftá cave houses and fabulous sunsets. Take time to admire the beauty of this enchanting island before retracing your steps and heading back to Crete via Théra.

Sunset at Oía: not to be missed

Shopping

Crete's four provincial capitals offer a huge range of choice, with scores of tiny hole-in-the-wall shops selling handmade leather goods, jewellery, textiles, ceramics and clothing, or village-made organic produce, such as honey, olive oil, dried herbs and nuts. Chaniá and Réthymno are especially pleasant towns in which to shop, because of their characterful traffic-free backstreets and large number of keen young artisans producing imaginative designs.

Iraklíon

Head straight for the market in Odós 1866 for the best choice in inexpensive souvenirs: herbs, leather, Cretan-style leather boots, jewellery, embroidery, dried figs, sponges, loofahs, etc. If you like Cretan music, look out for the Music Market on Odós 1821 (the street that runs parallel to the market. Also on Odós 1821 (at No 20) is Nick Papadogiannis, a more upmarket shop dealing in objets d'art – Minoan-style and modern statuary, pottery and jewellery.

Odós Kalokairinou is Iraklíon's principal shopping street – the place to go for clothes and everyday household goods. Odós 25 Augoústou contains a handful of interesting shops among the plethora of banks, car hire and travel agents: Eva Grimm (No 6) specialises in old Cretan handicrafts (antique woven cloth and wooden blocks for stamping biscuits, for example); George Mamouzelos (No 20) has a fascinating collection of sponges, and Minos

Cretan Wines (No 12) needs no further explanation.

Fashionable, upmarket clothing stores line the pedestrianised Odós Daidálos, and the side streets at its upper end are dominated by shops selling fine reproductions of Cretan icons and Minoan jewellery.

Ágios Nikólaos

Upmarket boutiques dominate this resort, but souvenir shops can also be found in the two streets that run uphill from the harbour. Starting with Odós 28 Octóbriou, look for No 14, Byzantio, which sells hand-painted icons copied from churches and monasteries. Chez Sonia, at No 20, sells antique Cretan costumes as well as unusual contemporary crafts and designs, including tapestries, puppets, ceramics and brasswork. On Odós Roussou Koundoúrou, Marisso (No 21) sells quality jewellery and, next door, Pegasus has antique jewellery and modern pieces incorporating ancient Greek coins.

Chaniá

Chaniá market hall makes a good starting point for a shopping expedition, though you may get no further as you linger over stalls laden with cheeses, herbs, honey, fish, fruit, meat and vegetables.

Leather Alley

Even more crowded and tempting is Odós Skridlóf, just down from the market, packed with stalls selling keenly priced leather bags, belts, sandals, wallets and shoes. Hidden among these, Tango (No 27) has some unusual jewellery and cast-glass lamps, No 31 sells DVDs and CDs of Cretan music, and Mares, opposite, sells camping, walking, fishing and snorkelling gear. If you fancy a pair of handmade knee boots, Cretan-shepherd style, look for the shop at No 67, but don't expect these to come cheap – they are made to last a lifetime.

Odós Khalídon

Cheap souvenirs account for most of the shops on this street, but do look out for colourful T-shirts, kaftans and beachwear at Nos 67 and 65. Opposite, Best is a browsing shop, full of colourful jewellery, painted wooden toys and boxes, and woven straw hats. In the former Turkish bath on the right, you can watch a bronze-caster at work making scales, weights, bells, candlesticks and door knockers.

Sponges are among the bargains to be had in Iraklíon's bustling market

To the fortress

The narrow alleys of the old Venetian quarter are dotted with shops selling the work of innovative young artists. Bizarro, on Odós Zambelioú, sells wacky waistcoats and blouses, plus exquisite puppets and dolls. On Odós Angeloú (running left from the entrance to the fortress), don't miss Top Hanao for their unrivalled selection of old Cretan rugs and tapestries.

Réthymno

Slightly more expensive and a touch more upmarket than Chaniá, Réthymno is packed with shopping temptations. Leading up to the fortress, Odós Salamínas has attracted young potters, painters and jewellers whose shops line both sides of the street. Odós Arambatzoglou is packed with shops such as The Link, for ethnic jewellery, Talisman for hanging lamps, and Dharma for handmade clothes. Also here is Olive Tree, selling furniture, jewellery and hair ornaments made of

You'll find lots of locally made pottery for sale in and around Chaniá

olive wood. In Odós Vernadou, which runs parallel, one block south, look for the Old Town Gallery, selling Judith Mooney's atmospheric watercolours of Cretan village life.

Odós Ethníkos Anistáseos is the main shopping street for locals, with a market at its upper end. For something truly local, Kogreion (No 41) sells worry beads in every imaginable colour and a ferocious array of knives. No 16 is a Dickensian antique shop where you may pick up an oil lamp among the miscellaneous junk. The little lane called Soulion has shops specialising in children's toys in painted wood and handmade dolls in Cretan costume.

Cretan Crafts

Some Cretan crafts – such as icon painting and jewellery making – have been revived in recent times by young, college-trained Cretans, keen to explore their ancient Minoan heritage. Their work is to be found in shops all over Crete and is remarkably good value. Other crafts, especially pottery and weaving, form part of a living tradition that has never died out, one that stems back 4,000 years to the Minoan era.

Pottery

Two villages specialise in the manufacture of pottery using timeless techniques. The potters of Margarítes, midway between Iráklion and Chaniá, supply many shops in Crete, but you can buy more cheaply, and watch the pots being made, by seeking them out at their source.

Ilias Ceramica, as you arrive, has the widest selection of pottery shapes and colours. For giant terracotta *pithoi*, just like those found in Minoan palaces, head through the village and out to Ceramica Kallerges (on the right) and Nickos Kaugalakis (further up on the left).

The other village, Thrapsanó, lies to the southeast of Iraklíon, near Myrtiá. Here the abundant red clay is simply scooped from the ground, shaped into *pithoi* and fired in wood kilns. At over 1m (3ft) tall, they do not make ideal souvenirs, but smaller pots can be found in the numerous shops in the village and lining the Kastélli road.

Weaving

Antique cloth and tapestries are richly coloured using vegetable dyes and decorated with simple geometric designs (good examples are displayed in the Museum of Cretan Ethnology in Vóroi – *see p64*). Woven from wool on a small horizontal loom, textile lengths are finished by knotting the warp threads and stitching lengths together to make bedspreads, knapsacks, saddle cloths and other items. Many towns in Crete sell woven bags and wall hangings, but to see the weavers at work, it is best to go to Anógia (east of Margarítes) or to Kritsá, on the hill to the southwest of Ágios Nikólaos.

The housefronts in both villages are hung from rooftop to pavement

Shoulder bags, Cretan style

with examples of weaving, which continue inside. The loom is often situated just inside the shop, so that the black-clad women weavers can rush out and commandeer any potential customers, sometimes physically pulling them in while keeping up a stream of sales patter in broken English or German.

Be prepared to be tough-skinned in seeking out precisely what you want and comparing prices before you buy. Do not pay over the odds for mass-produced rugs decorated with motifs from Minoan frescoes. On the other hand, do not expect genuine handmade textiles to come cheap. If you are easily intimidated by aggressive sales techniques, go instead to Top Hanao, the shop in Chaniá that specialises in genuine handwoven rugs and bedspreads.

Entertainment

Nightclubs abound in Crete's towns and holiday resorts, patronised as much by local youth as by holidaymakers. Other forms of entertainment are far harder to find on Crete, the choice often being limited to drama in the open-air theatres of Réthymno or Iraklíon (incomprehensible if you do not understand Greek), or rather traditional performances of Cretan music and dance, usually provided as part of a carefully packaged 'Cretan Evening' and heavily promoted by tour agents.

Nightlife

Cretan nightclubs are pretty relaxed by the standards that prevail in many European cities, although Cretans dress up. There is often only a minimum admission fee – the club makes its money from the sale of drinks but, this being Crete, the prices are not extortionate by any means. A popular activity is cruising from one club to the next, looking for the best party atmosphere.

Cretan music

An evening spent listening to authentic Cretan songs, variously jolly and wistful, plaintive and rambunctious, can be a memorable experience (if you drink too much *raki*, as you will surely be encouraged to do, you may also end up with a very memorable headache!). The melody in Cretan music is usually played on the three-stringed lyra, which sounds like a violin, accompanied by the flute, guitar, drum, bagpipes and the lute-like *bouzoúki*. Sometimes the

vocalist and lyra throw the tune about, taking it in turns to weave ever more complex variations, with the other instruments providing a driving rhythm that sounds like an Irish jig gone Arabic. Many tavernas offer live music as a background while you eat, but for a taste of the real thing, head for Café Crete, also known as the Lyrakia, at Odós Kalergon 22, Chaniá. This very basic hole-in-the-wall café behind the Arsenal is where Chaniá's traditional musicians gather for jam sessions and impromptu dancing. The atmosphere is warm and welcoming, especially on Friday night when hundreds of villagers descend on Chaniá for the next day's big street market.

Dancing

Chaniá is also one of the best places to watch traditional dancing from all over the Greek archipelago. The venue is the Firkás Theatre, the rather grand name given to the inner courtyard of the Old

Venetian Fortress at the northwestern tip of the harbour. Performances, lasting two hours, take place on some summer evenings, featuring 32 dances from different parts of Greece, each in appropriate costume. The admission ticket includes free *raki*.

Open-air cinema

Cretans are very fond of the cinema, and open-air screenings are commonplace in summer in the outdoor theatres in the fortresses at Chaniá and Réthymno, or in the lee of the city wall below the Archaeological Museum in Iraklíon. Screenings are in the original language, with Greek subtitles. Cretan audiences are very noisy, so you may need to listen hard to hear the dialogue. Look out for fly posters advertising these, and more conventional indoor screenings.

There's plenty of evening entertainment around the harbour in Ágios Nikólaos

EASTERN CRETE
Iraklíon and Iraklíon Province

Amnesia

One of the province's foremost nightspots, Amnesia has live DJs playing electronic dance music nightly.

Odós Agios Paraskévis 9, Chersonísou, Iraklíon. Tel: (28970) 25490. www.amnesiaclub.gr

Banana Club

Loud, lively and full of trendy young things, the new Banana Club is fast becoming one of Crete's legendary venues.

Odós Mália, Mália, Iraklíon. www.bananaclub.gr

Bio Bio

Electronic music and dancing until the early hours is the appeal of Bio Bio. Find it on the coast road through Chersonísou.

Odós Agios Paraskévis, Chersonísou, Iraklíon. www.biobio.gr

Enigma

A stylish club and one popular with locals as well as visitors, Enigma is known for its Greek-style disco-dance music.

Odós Agios Paraskévis 53, Chersonísou, Iraklíon. Tel: (28970) 23634.

Matrix Club

A spacious disco venue with a state-of-the-art sound system, this club is known for its hip hop, electro and house music.

Odós Eleftheriou Venizélou, Chersonísou, Iraklíon. Tel: (28970) 21103. www.matrixclub.gr

New York

One of the longest-established clubs along this coastline, the New York is a cool seafront eatery by day and a music and party venue by night.

Odós Agios Paraskévis 30, Chersonísou, Iraklíon. Tel: (28970) 23415. www.new-york.gr

Zig Zag

If you love garage, trance, house and R&B head for Zig Zag, one of Mália's top clubs. Enjoy cocktails and dancing until the small hours.

Odós Mália, Iraklíon. Tel: (2810) 343344. www.zigzagclub.gr

Lassíthiou Province

Armida

Anchored just off the quayside, this floating bar is one of the most atmospheric venues in town. Live music combines with colourful cocktails.

West Quay, Ágios Nikólaos

Pyramid

This Egyptian-themed bar provides snacks during the day and a place to relax listening to music in the evening. It overlooks the bay.

Sissi Bay, Lassíthiou. Tel: (28410) 71358.

WESTERN CRETE
Chaniá and Chaniá Province

Cosmos Piano Bar

A stylish venue looking out over the bay, this piano bar offers music, upmarket wines and around 300 different malts.

Pano Platanias, Chaniá. Tel: (69565) 65813.

Destijl Club

An atmospheric music club with a courtyard bar and dance area surrounded by palm trees.

Harbourside, Agia Marina, Chaniá.

Ela

The sound of live music and lively conversation

rings out from this bar-cum-taverna housed in a former soap factory.
Odós Kondilaki 47, Chaniá.
Tel: (28210) 74128.
www.ela-chania.gr

Knimatografos Music Café

By day this café serves snacks to background music and by evening is transformed into a lively place to dance.
Old Venetian Port, Chaniá.
Tel: (28210) 99293.

Mylos

In a period building yet somehow maintaining a chic feel, Mylos offers music and dancing into the small hours.
Harbourside, Kato Platanias, Chaniá.

Synagogi Bar

Located in the heart of the old town, this popular bar has period décor and a lively taste in music.
Odós Ar. Kondilaki, Chaniá Old Town.
Tel: (28210) 95242.

Réthymno and Réthymno Province

Brachos

Created within a cave right on Koube Beach, this super music bar plays genres from reggae and hard rock to local sounds.
Koube Beach, Réthymno.
Tel: (28310) 22680.

Figaro Art Cafe

With wall-mounted works of art and a drinks range that includes speciality coffees and cocktails, this café housed in a Venetian villa is chic and inviting.
Odós Xatziminali 22, Old Town, Réthymno.
Tel: (28310) 22334.
www.figarocafe.gr

Fortezza Club

Find this lively dance club in one of the stone buildings of the Venetian Port. International music presented by DJs is the speciality.
Odós Nearhou 14, Réthymno.
Tel: (28310) 55493.
www.fortezzaclub.gr

La Boheme

Enjoy Greek blonde and black draught beer, cocktails and delicious snacks in the courtyard of this town-centre venue.
Odós Souliou 15, Réthymno.
Tel: (69396) 59302.
www.laboheme.civila-rethymnon.com

Living Room

As its name suggests, this is a place to relax on big stylish sofas while enjoying a cocktail, nibbles and upbeat music well into the night.
Odós Eleftheriou Venizelou 5, Réthymno.
Tel: (28310) 21386.
www.living.com.gr

Metropolis

With Cretan and Latin theme nights and a host of drinks creations, this is one of Réthymno's most popular bars.
Odós Nearhou 12, Réthymno.
Tel: (69762) 93592.
www.metropolis-crete.com

Rock Café

Specialising in cocktails, this music bar's resident DJs play hard rock, R & B and pop as you dance the night away.
Odós Ioánnis Petihaki 1, Réthymno. Tel: (28310) 32118.

Rose Café Beach Bar

Located right by the beach, this bar offers a host of drinks for adults and a play area for youngsters.
Adelianos Kampos, Réthymno.
Tel: (28310) 72776.

Children

Almost nothing on Crete is geared specifically to children's tastes, and yet most children who come to the island on holiday succeed in having a marvellous time. In the process, however, their parents will probably end up being pestered to exhaustion by endless questions provoked by the magical strangeness of everything.

When visiting Crete with children, it is an advantage to choose a resort that has not been swamped by tourism, so that the everyday rhythms and activities of Cretan life can be allowed to take over. Many of the quieter resorts on the south coast – scarcely more than fishing villages – offer safe bathing, traffic-free streets and the chance to do and see things Cretan. Breakfast on creamy yoghurt flavoured with wild-flower honey, shop at the local bakers for fresh bread and syrup-soaked pastries, watch fishermen clean their catch and mend their nets, marvel at the myriad fish darting among the rock pools by the harbour, and say hello to the laden donkeys as they clip-clop mournfully up the street.

Archaeology and caves

To the horror of purists, most archaeological sites on Crete are unprotected from the erosive effects of visitors' feet and nobody seems to mind that hordes of visitors scramble over 4,000-year-old walls, staircases and courtyards. In fact, short of building a viewing platform above the site, it would be impossible to see the excavated remains without walking all over them. This presents a great opportunity for children who love exploring ruins and getting lost in the labyrinthine network of streets, corridors and storerooms making up a typical Minoan site. For added gloom, dankness and awesome rock formations, the Díktaean Cave (*see pp80–81*) is a must.

Beaches and watersports

The island offers dozens of sandy beaches and, for older children, a variety of watersports in the main resorts. Undercurrents are quite common and parents should keep a close watch on children swimming in the sea. Care should also be taken to protect children from the sun, particularly between 11am and 3pm when the sun is at its hottest. The island's four waterparks (*see p162*) provide hours of fun for children of all ages.

Boat trips

The seas around Crete are normally as calm as a pond (though they get rough as autumn sets in, from mid-October, and can continue choppy well into April). Well worth considering are the boat excursions from Ágios Nikólaos or Eloúnta out to Spinalónga Island (*see p87*), or the south-coast ferry service linking Palaióchora, Soúgia, Agía Rouméli, Loutró and Chorá Sfakion. For something less adventurous, but equally rewarding, go to Georgioúpoli (*see p125*) and hire a pedal boat for exploring the Almirós River, with its terrapins, crabs and rich birdlife.

Food

If you are travelling with children then the chances are they will need some persuasion to eat unfamiliar Cretan food. One answer could be to order a *mezédhes*. Typically comprising around 25 small dishes that are brought to your table a few at a time, a *mezédhes* starts with dips, warm pitta bread and Greek salad, and then progresses through a steady stream of local dishes. These might include grilled chicken, pork on skewers known as *souvláki*, slow-cooked lamb known as *kleftiko*, fish, stuffed vegetables and meatballs. *Sfakanies pites*, which are pastries drenched in honey, may complete the meal. From so much choice your children are sure to find something that suits their taste buds, but if all fails Crete also has its share of restaurants serving international cuisine.

Cafés and tavernas warmly welcome families with children

Sport and leisure

In the heat of a Cretan summer, few visitors to the island come with the objective of working out and limbering up. Crete caters more for the beach-loving sybarite than the fitness freak. However, organised sports are becoming available and many new pursuits, including golf, are planned to encourage tourists to come to Crete in winter.

Waterparks

There are now many waterparks to choose from, all offering a range of waterslides and other aquatic activities. Chersonísou, east of Iraklíon, has two: **Star Beach Waterpark** (*tel: (28970) 24472. www.starbeach.gr*) on Beach Road, with numerous sports facilities (waterskiing, windsurfing, parasailing and scuba diving among them) as well as rides, and **Aqua Plus** (*tel: (28970) 24950. www.acquaplus.gr*), located just to the north of Chersonísou on the Kastélli road. Midway between Iraklíon and Chersonísou at Anópoli, **Water City** (*tel: (2810) 781317. www.watercity.gr*) has 23 water slides. The latest waterpark is **Limnou Polis** (*tel: (28210) 33246. www.limnoupolis.gr*) at Varýpetro, 8km (5 miles) southwest of Chaniá.

Diving

The seas surrounding Crete are still relatively clean and teeming with fish, as anyone can tell just by looking into rock pools. This, and a sea floor covered in antiquities, means diving is very strictly controlled. Among the organisations licensed to train divers and take them on recreational trips to the seabed are **Atlantis Diving Centre** (*Grecotel, Adeloanos Kampos, Réthymno. Tel: (28310) 71640. www.atlantis-creta.com*) and the **Scuba Kreta Diving Club** (*Nana Beach Hotel, Chersonísou. Tel: (28970) 24076. www.scubakreta.gr*). Both provide English-speaking instructors and offer introductory dives of half a day or a day's duration, as well as four-day courses leading to the internationally recognised PADI diploma.

Beaches and watersports

Calm waters and a lack of wind do not make ideal windsurfing conditions, but equipment can be hired from local shops or from beachside huts in Almrída (*see pp124–5*) and Chersonísou (near Mália). In Palaióchora, the English-run Westwind Windsurfing School (located in a group of huts on the north end of the western beach) will supply boards, tuition and wetsuits, and they run their own rescue boat service.

Beach and watersport activities on Crete, in general, depend upon entrepreneurial young Cretans (or sometimes Germans or English) setting up a makeshift stall on the beach. The situation differs from year to year, but you are almost certain to find somebody offering the questionable pleasures of 'banana' rides, waterskiing and paragliding at Mália, Ágios Nikólaos and the resort strip west of Chaniá.

Beach etiquette

Topless bathing is widespread on Cretan beaches, and nude bathing, although officially illegal, is found in the less accessible coves and beaches of the south coast. If in doubt, take your cue from the behaviour of others on the beach. Once off the beach, however, you are expected to dress with decorum, and not to upset local sensibilities by walking around in revealing beachwear.

The beach at Chersonísou

The Cretan menu

The Cretan diet is the healthiest in the Western world – and that's official. Medical studies into the Mediterranean diet were actually conducted on Crete, where it was found that people lived longer, were healthier in old age, and suffered from less heart disease and cancer than in other parts of Europe and the Americas. The principal components of this diet, until quite recently, were bread in very large quantities, accompanied by olives, lots of fresh fruit and raw vegetables, olive oil, red wine, and protein in small quantities, principally in the form of goat's milk, cheese, walnuts or fish.

Fish, part of the national staple diet

Tavernas

The legacy of this peasant diet can still be found on the menu of a typical Cretan taverna where you can eat heartily, and cheaply, on Greek salad (tomatoes, onions, cucumber, olives and feta – sheep's milk cheese), followed by fresh fish, or any number of healthily lean high-fibre dishes, such as stuffed vine leaves (*dolmadákia*), bean soup (*soupa fassólia*) or so-called field vegetables (*agria hórta*), a salad made of wild leaves, most of them related to the dandelion.

'Comfort food'

Fortunately, Cretan tavernas offer a lot of comforting food as well: spinach and cheese pies (*spanakopopita/tiropitakia*) wrapped in filo pastry and oozing with flavour (and fat), for example, or macaroni and minced beef (*pastítsio*) baked with a rich cheese sauce, or aubergine and minced lamb moussaka.

Grilled foods

Charcoal-grilled lamb, chicken, pork chops and steak are commonplace, but *souvláki* remains the all-time favourite taverna dish, usually consisting of a barbecued pork kebab, though these days you will also find beef, lamb, mixed meats and fish *souvláki* on most menus. Country tavernas may offer rustic dishes, such as casserole of rabbit (*kounéli*), pigeon (*pitsounia*) or wild boar (*agrióhiros*), while every beachside restaurant worthy of its name will offer a tempting choice of grilled fresh fish, such as bream, bass, mullet, snapper, swordfish and (usually imported) lobster.

Sticky desserts

Tavernas do not, as a rule, serve desserts, though most will provide a bowl of delicious yoghurt with honey if asked, or a selection of fruit. For *baklavás* (filo pastry stuffed with honey and nuts) or *kadaifi* (shredded pastry filled with walnuts and syrup), it is traditional to move on to a specialist pastry shop cum café, known as a *zakaroplasteíon*. Here the cloying sweetness of the sticky pastries can be tempered by a strong Greek coffee (*métrio*, for medium sweet, *vari glikó* for sweet, *skéto* for without sugar), or a 'Nescafé' (the all-purpose term for all brands of instant coffee) served cold with a head of whipped milk, or hot with boiled milk.

Alcohol

Retsina – white wine flavoured with pine resin – is an excellent

Your choice of *oúzo*

accompaniment to Cretan food, but it is not a traditional Cretan wine. Some rural restaurants serve their own delicious home-made wine, drawing it directly from huge wooden barrels. Bottled local wines include Cava d'Or, Olympias, Gorthys, Tsantalia and Calliga, all of which are available in red, white or rosé versions. Cretan winemakers distil delicious *raki*, a clear aniseed-flavoured spirit, from the grape pips and skins left over from the wine-making process. An *ouzeri*, similar to a traditional café (*kafeníon*), serves the aniseed-flavoured aperitif known as *oúzo*, usually with little dishes of olives, cucumber, tomatoes or beans as an accompaniment.

Food and drink

Everywhere you go in Crete, even in the remotest villages, you are sure to find a simple taverna serving inexpensive home-cooked food, open from breakfast time to late at night. Tavernas are ubiquitous, but do not expect any great variety among the dishes on offer: menus are virtually identical, from one end of the island to the other.

How, then, do you select a taverna, especially when faced with the plethora of choice that exists in the popular resorts and in the harbour areas of Chaniá and Réthymno? Start by ignoring any restaurant that employs touts to attract custom, and treat with suspicion any that display glossy pictures illustrating the dishes on offer. These tourist tavernas are, on the whole, more expensive and worse value than the simple unpretentious tavernas used by local people. If you want a hearty Greek salad that clearly hasn't been portion-controlled, or a generous-sized swordfish steak, instead of a piece the size of a postage stamp, avoid the tourist areas. Be prepared to sacrifice the harbour views in favour of better value and better cooking in the backstreets and side alleys.

Menus

Restaurants in big towns will usually present a multilingual menu, but in village tavernas you may simply be taken to the kitchen and shown what is available. Menus will usually indicate whether fish is fresh or frozen. Most fresh fish is priced by the kilo and can be very expensive if you choose exotic varieties, such as lobster, but very good value if you stick to local fish. A red mullet or red snapper, for example, typically weighing 0.75kg (1½lb), makes a substantial and inexpensive meal for two.

Booking

Locals always book tables at good restaurants in Crete, however space will often be found for newcomers, even if it means bringing extra tables and chairs out. In any event, there is always another almost identical taverna next door.

Prices

Just as menus vary little, so prices are consistent across the island. The price of the meat will vary according to what you eat rather than where, with fresh fish being more expensive than meat, and baked or stuffed dishes being cheapest of all.

Some restaurants, especially those located in the provincial capitals, are trying to move upmarket, offering a more formal ambience than the traditional taverna. These are slightly more expensive and are indicated in the text by a ★★ symbol (three-course meal for two with local wine costing up to €26) as opposed to the ★ symbol (the same for up to €17).

Vegetarian food

Although Cretan food is dominated by fish and meat dishes, there are usually vegetarian options on most menus. Dishes like *briam* (a kind of ratatouille) and stuffed tomatoes, stuffed peppers and aubergines are all very tasty. Be sure to check they don't have meat in them, though, as they can be cooked both ways. No Cretan menu is complete without a long list of salads, either.

EASTERN CRETE
Iraklíon province
Agía Galíni

The little resort of Agía Galíni, about halfway along the south coast, has lots of good eating places. Below are just two of the best.

Charlie's Place ★ Fun place with bags of character, which doesn't even have a phone. Small menu but creative Cretan dishes.

Madame Hortense ★★ Some of the best food in town (try their chicken with

peas and olives), and tables overlooking the harbour are in great demand so get there early.

Ágios Giórgios

Dias ★ and Rea ★ Situated on the main street, these two restaurants serve local dishes (rabbit in season) and village wine, and make a good alternative to the more crowded restaurants of nearby Psychró.

Iraklíon

For all its size, Iraklíon does not have a huge choice of restaurants. For best value, head for Fotíou Theodosáki, the alley linking Odós 1866 and Odós Evans. The numerous and nameless tavernas here are busy with market customers and traders during the day and serve authentic Cretan baked dishes and roast meats.

Ligo Krasi, Ligo Thalassa ★ Packed most nights, this popular seafood

Seafood right by the sea, a Cretan treat

taverna, overlooking a busy intersection above the Venetian harbour, dishes up enormous portions of *mezédes* and freshly caught fried seafood at astonishingly low prices.
Corner I. Mitsotaki & Marineli (opposite Venetian harbour). Tel: (2810) 300501. Open: daily, all day.

Vizandio ★ The pavement tables sheltered by (plastic) vines and (real) bougainvillaea spill round into pedestrianised Odós Daidálou. Serves everything from inexpensive pasta and pizza to veal dishes and grilled meats.
Odós Byzántiou.

Brillant ★★ A local favourite, this stylish restaurant offers creative interpretations of traditional Cretan dishes using the finest Mediterranean products. Book in advance and dress up for the occasion.
Lato Hotel, Odós Epimenidou 15. Tel: (2810) 334959. www.brillantrestaurant.gr. Open: daily, lunch and dinner.

Erganos Tavern ★★ Full of atmosphere, this super taverna has the décor of a traditional Cretan village house. The menu has classic dishes like *dolmadákia* (stuffed vine leaves).
Georgiadi 5. Tel: (2810) 285629.

Ionia ★★ Popular with archaeologists since it was founded in 1923, the Ionia serves traditional Greek fare. The menu is based on what is fresh in the nearby market.
Odós Evans 3.

Loukoulos ★★ Serves a good range of authentic pizzas, cooked in a wood-fired brick oven, plus fish and vegetarian dishes.
Odós Koraí 5. Tel: (2810) 224435. www. loukoulos-restaurant.gr

O Kyriakos ★★ Smart and formal place, popular for special occasions. The *meze* spread is highly recommended.
Leofóros Dimokratías 53. Tel: (2810) 222464.

Parasies ★★ With a modernist yet cosy décor, this town-centre eatery serves upmarket classic

Cretan dishes with fine wines.
Odós Kalama. Tel: (2810) 225009.

Taverna Paralia ★★ Right by the water with views of the Venetian fortress, one of the best places to try fresh fish (and not too expensively).
Odós Venizélou 5.

Mália

Huge numbers of tavernas line the main street of this popular resort, most offering Cretan food tailored to British tastes. For something more authentic, head for nearby **Mílatos**, which has several very simple but good, reasonably priced restaurants serving fresh fish.

Mátala

The lovely beachfront is lined with west-facing tavernas, all with terraces designed to make the most of the views and the soothing sound of the breaking waves. All the tavernas specialise in fresh fish and there is little to choose between them.
Sirlaki ★, on the beach,

has a huge menu of pizzas, pasta, Greek dishes, grilled meat or fish and offers wine from the barrel. The less accessible **Skala** ★ fish taverna, just across the cliffs, is smaller and cheaper.

Myrtos

Taverna Akti ★ Fresh fish brought to your table, or slightly unusual dishes like octopus *stifadi*, set this taverna apart. It's at the far eastern end of the string of waterfront tavernas.
Tel: (28420) 51584.

Lassíthiou province

Ágios Nikólaos

Tourist-trap restaurants line the harbour and the south side of Lake Voulisméni. As always, the more interesting restaurants are located a block or so back from the seafront.

Dionysos ★★ The fish and seafood cuisine served at this stylish taverna that looks out over the lake has distinct Cretan and French influences.
Lake Ágios Nikólaos.
Tel: (28410) 25060.

La Casa ★ Seating by the lake and a menu ranging from simple snacks to full meals make this eatery a very popular spot.
28 Oktovriou 31.
Tel: (28410) 26362.

Meltemi ★★ Classy dining in the award-winning restaurant at the Istron Bay Hotel – worth the short drive out of town south along the coast to sample the imaginative cooking.
Istron Bay Hotel.
Tel: (28410) 61303.
www.istronbay.gr

Pacifae Restaurant ★★ This lakeside restaurant serves such Greek dishes as *kleftiko* (slow-cooked lamb) and *kounéli* (rabbit), along with fresh fish and seafood.
Lake Ágios Nikólaos.
Tel: (28410) 24466.

Pelagos ★★ Excellent fish tavern set in a neoclassical mansion, with a fishing boat in the front garden. Dine in the attractive rear garden. Good-value *fruits de mer* (seafood salad).
Odós Koráka 9. Tel: (28410) 25737.
www.pelagos.restaurant.gr

Eloúnta

Eloúnta's seafront is lined with restaurants all serving the same fish menus. The prices here, reflecting the cost of fresh seafood, tend to be higher than in many parts of Crete, but there are alternatives; plenty of places offer pasta, pizza or local *meze* dishes.

Ferryman ★ At the southern end of the waterfront, the Ferryman's menu is more imaginative than most in this resort. Try the Cretan lamb in red wine.
Harbourside.
Tel: (28410) 41230.

Marilena Restaurant ★★ A creative menu of Cretan and flambéed dishes combined with live Greek music and dancers in traditional dress make this a lively place to dine.
Harbourside.
Tel: (28410) 41322. www. marilenarestaurant.gr

Vritomartes ★★ Built on an artificial island in the harbour and selling unusual types of fish caught by the restaurant's own boat, this restaurant does decent Greek food at reasonable prices. *Tel: (28410) 41325.*

Ierápetra

Just up from the Venetian fortress, on Odós Samóyha, is **Phesteria ★** tavern, which prides itself on fresh fish grilled over charcoal. Further up the same street, all with beachside tables, are the **Ouseri Manos**, **Kyknos**, **Konaki**, **Napoleon** and **Sea Horse** (all ★), serving standard taverna fare at reasonable prices.

Káto Zákros
Káto Zákros Bay Restaurant ★ Family-run taverna right by the sea in this idyllic little spot, using ingredients from their own farm.

Sitía

Mixos ★ Much liked by locals, with imperious and unsmiling waiters (all part of the act) serving excellent grilled fish and chicken, spit-roasted over a glowing charcoal fire. Tables spill out on to the street in summer. *Odós Kornarou 112.*

Zorbas ★ This huge taverna, with tables on the harbour and round two other sides of the block, nevertheless offers snappy service. Visitors come for the huge plates of mixed *souvláki* or mixed grilled fish and for the the bustling atmosphere. *Odós Venizélou 64. Tel: (28430) 22689.*

The Balcony Restaurant ★★ With a small but creative menu with Asian and Greek influences, this is an upmarket eatery in the centre of town. *Odós Fountalidou 19. Tel: (28430) 25084. www. balcony-restaurant.com*

Tzermiádho
Kronio ★ Authentic Greek fare including *stifado* (meat stew), lamb with artichokes, *dolmadákia* (stuffed vine leaves), and cuttlefish with spices. *In the centre of the village.*

WESTERN CRETE
Chaniá province
Chaniá
Chaniá is the gourmet capital of Crete, with

scores of good tavernas lining the long harbour front, and as many more in the characterful alleys of the old city beneath the fortress. The waterfront restaurants divide roughly into three sections. Nearest the fortress (on Aktí Kountourioti) are the young, noisy, popular and reasonably cheap tavernas. Beyond the Mosque of the Janissaries (on Aktí Tombázi) are the quieter, more sophisticated places. Around and beyond the Arsenal buildings (on Aktí Enoseos) come the tavernas most favoured by local people – more typically Cretan in the informal and friendly management style.

Kariatis ★ Good-value pizzeria and *spaghetteria* favoured by students at the local Technical University. *Behind the Customs House in Plateía Katehaki.*

Monastiri ★ This down-to-earth taverna on the Old Harbour dishes up delicious Cretan specialities with names

like 'The Little Devil' (a long, spicy village sausage) and 'The Nun's Mistake' (a dish of succulent pork chops)! Also try the mouthwatering lamb in oil and wine.
Aktí Tompazi 12.
Tel: (28210) 55527.
www.monastiri-
taverna.gr.
Open: daily, all day.

Apostolis ★★ This locally favoured, family-owned seafood taverna serves unusually generous fish portions. The attention to detail is impressive – from the fresh-out-of-the-oven hot bread and olive oil to the complimentary dessert and *oúzo* at the end.
Aktí Enoseos 10.
Tel: (28210) 43470. www. apostolisrestaurants.gr.
Open: lunch till late.

Belvedere Restaurant ★★ A signature dish of *stifado* (beef) with a twist, fine wine and Greek music set this restaurant apart. Great views over the harbour.
Ano Platanias.
Tel: (28210) 60003.

Dinos ★★ Justifiably popular seafood taverna.

Fine views of the harbour.
Odós Enoseos, on the corner with Odós Sarpidóna.
Tel: (28210) 41865.

Nykterida ★★ Well worth the taxi ride from Chaniá, both for the food and garden setting. Occasional local music and dancing.
Korákies (a village 5km/ 3 miles east of Chaniá).
Tel: (28210) 64215.

Remezzo Restaurant ★★ Serving informal meals by day and classic dishes and cocktails by night, Remezzo is a landmark eatery right on the harbourside.
Plateía Eleftheriou Venizélou 16A,
Old Port.
Tel: (28210) 52001.
www.remezzo-crete.gr

Ristorante Italiano Veneto ★★ Housed in a renovated 15th-century Venetian building, this chic eatery has a menu offering Italian pasta, pizza and à la carte dishes, accompanied by fine wines.
Odós Zamepliou 8.
Tel: (28210) 93527.
www.venetorestaurant.gr

Safran ★★ This chic restaurant in a renovated warehouse on the waterfront has quickly developed a reputation for serving up superb contemporary Greek-cum-Mediterranean cuisine. Try the signature Flambé Shrimps in *Oúzo* and Saffron.
Akti Tompazi 30.
Tel: (28210) 56333.
www.safranchania.com.
Open: Tue–Sun, lunch & dinner.

Several restaurants in Chaniá have attractive patios or pleasantly shaded courtyard gardens

Tamam ★★ Popular taverna converted from the old Turkish baths. Basement interior is simple but atmospheric. Tables spill on to the pavement in summer. Cheap house wine straight from the barrel.
Odós Zambelioú 49.
Dinner only.
Tel: (28210) 96080.

Well of the Turk ★★★ Cellar taverna with spicy food and Arabic music.
Kalinikou Zarpáki 1. Tel: (28210) 54547.
www.welloftheturk.com

Georgioúpoli

Almiros ★ The town's best restaurant, with an extensive range of good-value dishes.
On the south side of the main square.

Poseidon ★ Rough and ready taverna, reached down a 100m (330ft) long path, serving absolutely fresh fish caught by local fishermen.
On the right-hand side of the road leading out to the National Highway.

Rodaria Restaurant ★★ This super little restaurant oozes charm and has a menu of pizza, pasta and Greek dishes like moussaka to tempt your taste buds.
Apokoronoy.
Tel: (28250) 61360.
www.rodaria.gr

Kolymvári

Locals come to Kolymvári from all over Crete for seafood dishes. Try the **Spatha** ★★ taverna (on the eastern side of the main square), with its garden terrace and sea views, or the **Diktina** ★ and **Argedina** ★ tavernas, facing each other further north on the Moní Gonías road, beyond the post office.

Palaióchora

Many of Palaióchora's restaurants are grouped round the central crossroads and the tables spill over the narrow pavements on to the road, causing havoc if any vehicle tries to get through.

Akropolis Ouzeri ★ A thoroughly Cretan establishment, very plain and functional, serving local sausages and rabbit.
On the crossroads in the centre of the town.

Caravella ★ Specialises in freshly caught fish with tables right on the foreshore.
By the ferry harbour.
Tel: (28230) 42354.
www.caravella.gr

Elite ★ Worth seeking out on Saturday nights for its Cretan music and dancing.
At the far end of the western beach road, beyond the Hotel Elma.

Galaxy Fish Restaurant ★★ In a place like this all you need to see on the

Taking a rest in the backstreets of Chaniá

menu is 'fresh fish from Palaióchora' to know it should be good, and it is. It's opposite the pebble beach at the eastern end of town.

Tel: (28230) 41059.
www.chaniagalaxy.com

The Third Eye ★
Imaginative vegetarian dishes.

Close to the westernmost of the two beaches.
Tel: (28230) 41234. www.
thethirdeye-paleochora.com

Vámos peninsula
Demetros ★ Fresh fish served on a terrace literally metres away from the sea, a romantic (and peaceful) spot at night.

Almrída, north of Kalíves.

Réthymno province
Réthymno
Avoid the multitude of overpriced restaurants lining the Aktí Venizélou beach road, and head for the Venetian Harbour, which has a good choice of seafood restaurants, or the alleys leading off Odós Arambatzoglou, where the pavement tables turn the whole area into one big outdoor party at night.

Famagusta ★ Try this Cypriot-owned restaurant if you are fed up with the usual Cretan fare. As well as Cypriot dishes, curries, stir-fried dishes and Japanese *teriyaki* are on the menu, and the special list of children's dishes features home-made fish fingers.

Plateía Plastera 6 (west of the Venetian Harbour).
Tel: (28310) 23881.

Myrogdies ★ Young owner-chef Nikos Nektarios sends light Mediterranean-style dishes out of the kitchen alongside more rustic local fare – either way, many of the plates feature pomegranates (the name of the taverna). The live music is as memorable as the food.

Odós E Vernadou 32. Tel: (69726) 95170. Open: nightly.

Ousies: Meze & Spirits ★
A local institution, this is one of Réthymno's most enjoyable ouzeries. Order half a dozen *mezédhes* and a bottle of *oúzo* and settle in for the night. Opt for Cretan specialities such as

Buyiurdi, a casserole of layered feta and fresh tomatoes.

Odós E Vernadou 20.
Tel: (28310) 56643.
Open: nightly.

Alana Restaurant ★★
Cretan cuisine and a host of à la carte Mediterranean dishes and fine wines can be enjoyed at this restaurant in the heart of the old town.

Odós Salaminos 15. Tel: (28310) 27737.
www.alana-restaurant.gr

Avli ★★ Very elegant restaurant within an old Venetian manor house. Try baby lobster in shrimp sauce, baked lamb in egg lemon sauce and casseroled goat. Delightful courtyard meals alfresco.

Odós Xanthoudídou 22.
Tel: (28310) 58250.
www.avli.gr

To Pigadi Restaurant ★★
You can dine alfresco on classic Cretan dishes like *pitsounia* (pigeon) at this restaurant housed in a 16th-century building next to the fortress.

Odós Xanthoudidou 31.
Tel: (28310) 27522.

Hotels and accommodation

Crete offers a huge range of accommodation, from simple 'rent rooms' in someone's home to luxurious self-contained resorts with private beaches, shops, restaurants and sports facilities. Most middle-range accommodation is located in small hotel or villa complexes where you can expect a simply furnished room with en-suite shower and toilet, a balcony for enjoying the sun, and sometimes a small kitchen for preparing light meals.

Hotels

Greek hotels are classified into six categories (luxury, A, B, C, D and E) according to the standard of facilities and services on offer. Unless you want to live in the lap of luxury, A and B class hotels are adequate and comfortable. Room prices are fixed according to the hotel's classification, but hoteliers will often (quite legitimately) get round this by charging for a whole range of extras, especially during the high season. You may find, for example, that the hotel charges you extra if you only stay one night; it can also insist on charging you for breakfast, or even for half board (breakfast and either lunch or dinner) even if you do not want to eat in the hotel. The lower-category hotels do not usually have restaurants and so cannot do this. Some will levy a charge for supplying a television in your room or present you with a bill for electricity consumed by central heating or air-conditioning systems, so make sure you know what the likely cost is to be in advance.

Villas and self-catering

Many package-tour companies offer accommodation in villa complexes rather than hotels, and these are not subject to the same degree of government control, so you cannot always be sure of the facilities on offer. A key point to check before you book is the availability of heating and air conditioning. Many villas have no heating, and this can result in a miserable holiday spent searching for warmth if, as can happen in April and October, cold and wet weather sets in. Conversely, you may be glad of something more than an open window for keeping cool during the intense heat of a Cretan summer.

Rent Rooms

Private accommodation, known universally on Crete as 'Rent Rooms', can be had in every tiny village. Traditionally, the family rented out spare rooms in their homes, but today's rent rooms are more likely to be in purpose-built blocks, equipped with kitchens and showers. Prices vary greatly, so you should shop around. It is accepted that you will want to see your room before agreeing to take it, and bargaining over the price is normal practice during the less busy seasons. Best discounts are given to people who intend to stay three days or more, and some owners may not be willing to rent rooms for a stay of only one night.

Go as you please

Most visitors to Crete base themselves in one place for a week or more, and travellers touring the island, staying at a different place each day, are still something of an oddity. Touring during the high season (July, August and early September) is made more difficult by the fact that most accommodation is pre-booked by tour operators. Touring in the spring and autumn is perfectly feasible, however, and you can sometimes secure big discounts on room rates from hoteliers keen for your custom.

Camping

There are about 20 official campsites on Crete (see *http://interhike.com* for details), and the standard is generally good. Legally you must use an official campsite, but in practice many visitors camp rough, near beaches and so on. It is not usually a problem, provided you are discreet, but there are occasional clampdowns and you must move on to an official campsite if instructed by the police.

Opt for a luxury hotel and enjoy the indulgence of a private beach

★   Less than €50
★★ €50–200
★★★ More than €200

EASTERN CRETE
Iraklíon province
Castro Amoudara ★
With a swimming pool, luxuriant gardens and its own taverna serving delicious Cretan cuisine, this 52-room hotel is good value for money.
Odós A Papandreou 301, Amoudara, Iraklíon. Tel: (2810) 822770. www.castro-hotel.com

Philoxenia Hotel ★
A pleasingly presented hotel with modern guestrooms looking out over the gardens and swimming pools. It is minutes from the beach and the centre of Mália.
Odós El Venizelou, Mália. Tel: (28970) 32081. www.philoxenia-malia.com

Albatros Hotel ★★
A wide range of amenities that include a children's club, fitness suite and restaurant ensures this remains one of the area's top hotels.
Odós Deadalou 1, Chersonísou. Tel: (28970) 22144. www.albatros.gr

Fodele Beach and Water Park ★★
This all-inclusive five-star holiday resort overlooking the beach and bay has its own waterpark, children's club and fitness centre. Guest accommodation includes bungalows in the gardens.
Fodele Beach, Iraklíon. Tel: (2810) 522000. www.fodelebeach.gr

Galaxy Hotel ★★★
Sleek and stylish, the Galaxy is one of Crete's finest hotels and has hosted world leaders. Guests can enjoy a wellness centre, gourmet restaurants and luxurious guestrooms.
Leoforos Dimokratias 75, Iraklíon. Tel: (2810) 238812. www.galaxy-hotel.com

Hersonisso Palace ★★★
A 150-room hotel in lush gardens, the Hersonisso Palace offers guests Greek-Mediterranean cuisine served in its restaurant, exercising in its fitness suite, swimming and tennis.
Limin Chersonísou, Chersonísou. Tel: (28970) 23603. www.hersotels.gr

Lassíthiou province
Camping Gournia Moon ★
This well-equipped campsite has pitches for tents, caravans and motorhomes, with on-site facilities including a restaurant. A short drive from Ágios Nikólaos.
Gourniá, Ierápetra, Lassíthiou. Tel: (28420) 93243.

Maritimo Beach Hotel ★★
Fresh, modern guestrooms and on-site amenities that include a sea-view restaurant, pool and terrace, traditional Cretan taverna and extensive gardens.
Sisi Bay, Lassíthiou. Tel: (28410) 71645. www.maritimo.gr

Eloúnta Bay Palace ★★★
Looking out over the picturesque bay, this luxurious hotel offers, a Thalasso spa, fitness suite and a restaurant famed for its seafood. A children's club is provided for family guests.
Mirabéllo Bay, Eloúnta. Tel: (28410) 67000. www.eloundabay.gr

WESTERN CRETE
Chaniá province
Arkadi Hotel ★

A stylish hotel, the Arkadi is located minutes from the old Venetian Harbour and town centre. Among its features are 64 air-conditioned guestrooms, lounge bar and café, and underground parking.
Plateía 1866, Chaniá.
Tel: (28210) 90181.
www.arkadi-hotel.gr

Grammeno Camping ★

Located just minutes from the beach, this is one of the largest and best-equipped campsites on Crete. Facilities include laundry, Internet connection, sunbeds and children's playground.
Kountoura, Palaióchora.
Tel: (28230) 42125. www.
grammenocamping.gr

Belmondo Hotel ★★

With a décor of wood complemented by Mediterranean colours and antique-style furniture, this is a hotel with immense character. It is housed in an original harbourside building. Breakfast is served in its courtyard.
Odós Zampetiou 10,
Chaniá.
Tel: (28210) 36216.
www.belmondohotel.com

Caretta Beach ★★

Standing in gardens surrounded by groves, this collection of apartments is designed for luxurious independent holidays. Facilities inlcude a private kitchenette and lounge with Internet connection, plus pools and an à la carte restaurant.
Platanías Gerani, Chaniá.
Tel: (28210) 61700.
www.caretta-beach.gr

Panorama Hotel ★★★

As its name suggests, the Panorama has great views from most rooms out over the ocean. On-site, there are two pools, a gymnasium and tennis courts for the energetic, a health spa and gourmet restaurants.
Kato Galatas, Chaniá.
Tel: (28210) 31700
www.panorama-hotel.gr

Réthymno province
Réthymno Youth Hostel ★

This youth hostel housed in a Venetian stone building in the heart of Réthymno is a great place to stay for anyone on a budget. Rooms are dormitory style, while amenities include fast Internet and showers. Breakfast and snacks are available.
Odós Tobazi 41,
Réthymno.
Tel: (28310) 22848.
www.yhrethymno.com

Avli Suites Hotel ★★

Housed in a Venetian building, this is one of the town's premier places to stay. Gorgeous guestrooms are complemented by its wine bar, rooftop spa and stylish courtyard restaurant.
Odós Xanthoudidou 22,
Réthymno. Tel: (28310)
58250. www.avli.gr

Palazzino di Corina ★★★

With their feature stone walls and rich fabrics, the apartments at this town-centre hotel in a converted Venetian building ooze luxury. Some even have four-poster beds and spa bathrooms. The hotel has a courtyard with a pool.
Odós Dambergi,
Réthymno. Tel: (28310)
21205. www.corina.gr

Practical guide

Arriving

By air

Scores of tour operators sell package tours to Crete, and if it is a combination of flight, transfers and accommodation you are looking for then this is by far the cheapest way of holidaying on the island. Low-cost airlines fly to Crete and are a good option if you wish to make your own travel and accommodation arrangements. Flight-only deals on charter flights are also available. Scheduled flights into Crete are expensive and involve a change of plane and terminal at Athens' airport. Check *www.flythomascook.com* for flights to Iraklíon. Alternatively, consider arriving in Crete the traditional way – by ferry from Piréas (the port of Athens).

Visas

US and Commonwealth nationals can stay in Crete for up to three months without a visa. Officially, to stay longer, you should apply to the tourist police for a visa, providing evidence that you can support yourself. EU nationals do not need a visa to stay on Crete.

Airport facilities

The main point of entry is the airport at Iraklíon, 5km (3 miles) east of the city centre. Rebuilt in 1995, this is a modern, relatively efficient airport with the usual facilities.

A few tour operators also use the small, recently upgraded airport near Chaniá. This is useful if you are staying in the west of the island. The airport at Sitía, in the east, is slowly being expanded.

Onward travel

Tour operators meet their customers at the airport and arrange onward travel by coach or taxi. If you are on your own, you can also take a taxi – the fares from the airport to the main destinations around the island are fixed, but it is wise to double-check and agree the fare in advance to avoid arguments at the other end. From Iraklíon airport, buses leave every few minutes for the city centre; from Chaniá airport, buses meet incoming flights, but many people take taxis.

By sea

Separate ferries ply daily across the Sea of Crete between the ports of Piréas and Iraklíon, Chaniá and Réthymno. Minoan high-speed ferries now take only six hours to Piréas and, if you are touring Greece, this is a remarkably cheap way to bring your car across. Travel agents in any Greek city will handle bookings – be sure to get the direct sailings, rather than those that stop at various islands, unless you want to double the journey time.

The Thomas Cook publication *Greek Island Hopping* has details of ferry times and can be purchased from *www.thomascookpublishing.com*, Thomas Cook branches in the UK or by telephoning *00 44 1733 416477*.

Camping

Crete has some 20 or so official camping sites, graded A (luxury) to C (basic), and a complete list can be obtained from tourist offices in Crete. You need not limit yourself to these, however, because although camping in the wild is against the law in Greece, plenty of enterprising farmers and landowners have put up 'Camping' signs on their land (especially on the roads leading to the popular beaches). In return for a small fee they will supply water and use of a kitchen, toilet and shower.

Children

Children are universally adored in Crete, and taking yours on holiday will guarantee that you make lots of friends. On the other hand, Cretan children are treated as mini-adults, expected to eat the same food, and stay up as late as grown-ups. Children's menus in tavernas are not common, but there is usually something they will readily eat (*see also pp160–61*).

Climate

The peak tourist season, from June to September, is very hot and dry, and the sun is intense. Spring (April and May) is delightful, with flower-filled meadows and warm, but not searing, sunshine.

Autumn begins in October and is marked by occasional downpours that can last a day or an hour, interspersed by days of brilliant blue skies and sunshine. Visiting Crete at this time of year can be a gamble because of the rain, but the island is becoming more popular as a winter holiday destination, where it is possible to ski in the mountains during the day and eat outdoors by the coast in the evening – in winter the temperature by the sea rarely drops below 8°C (46°F) and is often considerably warmer.

Conversion tables

See p181.

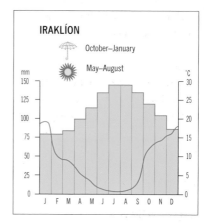

WEATHER CONVERSION CHART

25.4mm = 1 inch

°F = 1.8 × °C + 32

Clothes and shoe sizes in Crete generally follow the standard sizes used in the rest of Europe.

Crime

Blissfully, Crete is relatively crime-free, and the only antisocial behaviour you are likely to encounter is from other visitors. Even here, the lager louts stick to their own haunts, and if you avoid late-night bars you are not likely to be troubled by their hooligan behaviour.

Despite the lack of crime, you should not be complacent – look after your valuables and do not leave them where a thief might be tempted; you can always use the hotel lockers.

Customs

There are no customs restrictions on the import and export of duty-paid purchases between Crete and other parts of the European Union. Be sure to check the customs regulations for your own part of the world before travelling. Some countries, including the USA, have far stricter limits on what may be imported from Crete.

Cycling

Crete is becoming increasingly popular among the mountain-bike fraternity, with plenty of testing dirt roads, as well as rock-paved tracks, to explore. Mountain bikes can be hired in all the main tourist centres. If the mountainous terrain puts you off, join an organised tour where bikes and cyclists are transported up the mountain, enabling you to enjoy the scenic ride downhill.

Driving

Cretans like to boast about their dare-devil driving skills but in reality it is only the taxi drivers and a few flash drivers of expensive cars that behave badly on the roads of Crete. Most people stick to a sedate speed (forced to do so by the steep, twisting terrain) except on the main east–west National Highway, where locals often break the official speed limit (90kph/56mph) and overtake on bends.

The National Highway is the island's main artery, running east–west across the top of the island. It is a good wide road but, despite appearances, it is not a dual carriageway. The right-hand lane is only used if you want to pull over to let a faster car past – it combines the functions of a crawler lane and hard shoulder. It is not a continuous carriageway, and disappears altogether from time to time. You may also find vehicles, flocks of sheep and roadside stalls blocking this lane.

The island's other roads all feed into the National Highway, running north, or – more often – south from it. These roads vary in quality from fast, wide, metalled roads with few bends to dirt tracks with massive potholes. However, many of the worst roads are currently being resurfaced. In general, roads running south are steep, twisting and slow-going.

During the rainy season (late October to early April), expect rock falls, landslides and occasionally snow to hamper your progress and be very wary of driving over rough roads – it is easy to damage the rim of your wheels and end up with a flat tyre. Where there is only room for one car to pass, the Cretans tend to be aggressive; it is wise to let Cretans go first, but do not flash your lights to indicate that you are giving way – on Crete, flashed lights mean 'get out of the way, I'm coming through!'

Practicalities

There are almost as many car rental agencies on Crete as there are restaurants and bars, so shop around for the best all-in deal – that is, one that includes comprehensive insurance, collision damage waiver and no mileage charges.

Drive on the right, wear seat belts in front and rear seats, and observe the speed limits: 50kph (31mph) in towns, 70kph (43mph) on ordinary roads, and 90kph (56mph) for cars, 70kph (43mph) for other vehicles, on the National Highway. Drunken driving is severely penalised. Petrol stations are ubiquitous and open long hours. Road signs are in English and Greek except in out-of-the-way places.

Electricity

Standard two-pin continental-type plugs are used on Crete and the supply is 220 volts/50 cycles. Visitors from the UK and the USA/Canada need an adaptor.

Practical guide

CONVERSION TABLE

FROM	TO	MULTIPLY BY
Inches	Centimetres	2.54
Feet	Metres	0.3048
Yards	Metres	0.9144
Miles	Kilometres	1.6090
Acres	Hectares	0.4047
Gallons	Litres	4.5460
Ounces	Grams	28.35
Pounds	Grams	453.6
Pounds	Kilograms	0.4536
Tons	Tonnes	1.0160

To convert back, for example from centimetres to inches, divide by the number in the third column.

MEN'S SUITS

UK	36	38	40	42	44	46	48
Rest of Europe	46	48	50	52	54	56	58
USA	36	38	40	42	44	46	48

DRESS SIZES

UK	8	10	12	14	16	18
France	36	38	40	42	44	46
Italy	38	40	42	44	46	48
Rest of Europe	34	36	38	40	42	44
USA	6	8	10	12	14	16

MEN'S SHIRTS

UK	14	14.5	15	15.5	16	16.5	17
Rest of Europe	36	37	38	39/40	41	42	43
USA	14	14.5	15	15.5	16	16.5	17

MEN'S SHOES

UK	7	7.5	8.5	9.5	10.5	11
Rest of Europe	41	42	43	44	45	46
USA	8	8.5	9.5	10.5	11.5	12

WOMEN'S SHOES

UK	4.5	5	5.5	6	6.5	7
Rest of Europe	38	38	39	39	40	41
USA	6	6.5	7	7.5	8	8.5

A fishing boat well equipped for the catch

Embassies

There is a British consulate at *Papalexándrou 16, Iraklíon (tel: (2810) 224012)*, but most other embassies are in Athens. If you need help, go to the tourist police in the first instance (*see* Police, *p187*).

Emergency telephone numbers

General *112*
Police *100*
Ambulance *166*
Fire *119*
Mountain Rescue *119*
Road Assistance *104*

Health

The greatest hazards to health on Crete are the sun, sea creatures and mosquitoes. It is very easy to burn in the sun, even just walking around, and even in the relatively mild spring weather, especially if you are exploring archaeological sites on exposed hillsides – wear a hat to protect your head and neck, and cover your arms. Jellyfish can give you a nasty nettle-like sting that takes up to a week to go down. There is no cure but patience and time, though the ammonia in urine is said to have a mildly relieving effect. Sea urchin spines are a greater hazard – these black creatures inhabit rocky shorelines and are nearly invisible against the rock, so always wear shoes or sandals when exploring rock pools. Spines can be extracted, like splinters, using a needle, but seek medical help if they go deep – they can go septic if not removed.

The most effective mosquito deterrents are the plug-in electrical devices that are widely available on Crete. The green pyrethrum insect repellent coils (*spíres* in Greek) are also fairly effective, but by no means foolproof, so take insect repellent cream.

Basic emergency care is free and there are good health clinics providing outpatient services from 8am to noon in every large town. These are signposted (with a red cross) and are easy to find.

EU residents should obtain a European Health Insurance Card (available online at *www.ehic.org.uk*, from the post office or *tel: 0845 606 2030*) before travelling. As this does not cover all health costs and never covers repatriation costs, it is advisable to take out adequate travel insurance as well.

Language

Cretans are great Anglophiles, and they watch English and American television programmes, so almost everyone speaks basic English. Even so, the ability to read

A bell tower silhouetted against the setting sun

Bartholomew Crete Holiday Map. For walking, it is best to use the excellent *Harms Verlag* 1:100,000 two-map set, which shows most of the footpaths. They are not widely available on Crete, so it is best to order them from a specialist map shop before you go.

Media

All your favourite newspapers (and many magazines) are sold on Crete, the day after publication. Cretan TV broadcasts many films and programmes in English (with Greek subtitles) and one channel is devoted to USA news.

Money and tax

The euro (€) is the unit of currency used in Crete. There are seven denominations of the euro note: €5, €10, €20, €50, €100, €200 and €500; eight denominations of coins: 1 cent, 2 cents, 5 cents, 10 cents, 20 cents, 50 cents, and €1 and €2.

Money-changers are ubiquitous, and some operate round the clock in big resorts. Commission rates vary enormously and it's worth shopping around to see who offers the best combination of exchange rate and commission. The worst rates are generally those of travel agents and hotels. Government tourist offices offer exchange facilities with rates that are similar to or lower than those of banks.

Major credit cards are accepted in main hotels, shops and restaurants, but not in cheap tavernas.

(*Cont. on p186*)

Greek characters and speak a few words will enrich your visit (*see pp184–5*).

Lost property

Cretans are instinctively honest and helpful and will turn in anything they find that they recognise to be important or valuable. Go to the tourist police if all else fails.

Maps

The best general maps of Crete currently available are the *Nelles* and *Freytag & Berndt* maps and the

Language

It is helpful to know the Greek alphabet so that you can recognise place names, while the few words and phrases following the alphabet will also come in handy. Take care to get the stress right: every Greek word has an accent (´) over the stressed syllable, and if you get it wrong you are not likely to be understood.

THE GREEK ALPHABET

Greek	Name	Pronounced
Α α	alpha	a
Β β	beta	b
Γ γ	gamma	g, but becomes y in front of e and i
Δ δ	delta	d
Ε ε	epsilon	e as in extra
Ζ ζ	zeta	z
Η η	eta	e as in eat
Θ θ	theta	th
Ι ι	iota	i
Κ κ	kappa	k
Λ λ	lambda	l
Μ μ	mu	m
Ν ν	ni	n
Ξ ξ	xi	x
Ο ο	omicron	o
Π π	pi	p
Ρ ρ	rho	r
Σ σ	sigma	s
Τ τ	taf	t
Υ υ	ypsilon	u
Φ φ	phi	ph
Χ χ	chi	ch as in loch
Ψ ψ	psi	ps
Ω ω	omega	long o

BASIC VOCABULARY

good morning	kaliméra
good evening	kalispéra
goodnight	kaliníkhta
hello	yásou
thank you	efkharistó
please/you're welcome	parakaló
yes	né
no	óchi
where is...?	pou iné?
how much is...?	póso káni?
do you speak English?	miláte angliká?
I don't speak Greek	dhen miló elinika
good afternoon	kaliapógevma
goodbye	antío
cheers!	gia mas!
okay	entáxei
sorry	signómi
help	voítheia
where is the nearest hospital?	poú eínai to plisiéstero nosokomeio?

FOOD AND DRINK

food	fagitó
bread	psomí
water	neró
wine	krasí
beer	bira
coffee	kafé
lobster	astakós
squid	kalamária
octopus	oktapódhi
red mullet	barboúnia
whitebait	marídhes
lamb	arnáki
chicken	kotópoulo
meat balls	keftédhes
skewered meat	souvlákia
pork	chirini
spinach	spanáki
courgette	kolokíthia
beans	fasoles
chips	patátes tiganítes
cucumber	angouri

FOOD AND DRINK (CONTINUED)

tomato	tomáta
olives	elíes
salad with feta	horiatíki
tomato salad	saláta
yoghurt cucumber dip	tsatsíki
black coffee	kafé skétos
coffee with milk	kafé ma gala

PLACES

street	odós
square	plateía
avenue	leofóros
room	dhomátio
post office	tachidhromió
police	astinomía
pharmacy	farmakío
doctor	iatrós
bank	trápeza
café	kafeníon
beach	paralía
bus station	stathmós
castle	kástro
church	ekklisía
island	nisí
monastery	moní
museum	mouseió
port	limáni
river	potámi
theatre	théatro

MONTHS

January	Ianouários
February	Fevrouários
March	Mártios
April	Aprílios
May	Máios
June	Ioúnios
July	Ioúlios
August	Avgoustos
September	Septémvris
October	Októvrios
November	Noémvrios
December	Dekémvrios

DAYS OF THE WEEK

Monday	Deftéra
Tuesday	Tríti
Wednesday	Tetárti
Thursday	Pémpti
Friday	Paraskeví
Saturday	Sávvato
Sunday	Kyriakí

COLOURS

black	mávro
green	prásino
red	kókkino
white	lefkó
yellow	kítrino

NUMBERS

1	éna	15	dekapénte	100	ekató
2	dhío	16	dekaéxi	200	diakósia
3	tria	17	dekaeptá	1000	chília
4	téssera	18	dekaochtó	2000	dýo chiliádes
5	pénde	19	dekaennéa		
6	éxi	20	eíkosi		
7	evtá	21	eikosiéna		
8	okhtó	30	triánta		
9	enéa	40	saránta		
10	dhéka	50	penínta		
11	énteka	60	exínta		
12	dódeka	70	evdomínta		
13	dekatía	80	ogdónta		
14	dekatéssera	90	enenínta		

As in all EU countries, visitors from outside the EU can reclaim the Value Added Tax (VAT) on high-value purchases – ask about the Tax Free Shopping scheme.

If you need to transfer money quickly, you can use the MoneyGram[SM] Money Transfer service. For more details in the UK, telephone Freephone *0800 8971 8971*.

The Thomas Cook website, at *www.thomascook.com*, provides up-to-the-minute details of Thomas Cook's travel services.

National holidays

Offices, banks and some shops close on national holidays, though in tourist resorts it is business as usual as long as there is money to be made. The dates of Lent, Easter and other religious holidays in the Orthodox calendar vary from year to year and can be up to two weeks later in the year than the equivalent feasts in the Western Church calendar.

New Year's Day 1 January
Epiphany 6 January
Clean Monday Variable – two days before Ash Wednesday
Independence Day 25 March
Good Friday Variable
Easter Monday Variable
Labour Day 1 May
Ascension Day Variable
Whit Monday Variable
Assumption Day 15 August
Okhi ('No') Day 28 October
Christmas Day 25 December
St Stephen's Day 26 December

Opening hours

Museums and archaeological sites

Opening hours vary considerably and change with alarming frequency. Most museums and sites are open all day every day in summer, although a few close at 3pm and all day on Monday. Opening hours are shorter in winter.

Shops

Stores catering to tourists typically open 10am–10pm, or later. Street kiosks stay open even longer. Shops and markets catering to the local population open 8am–1.30pm Monday to Saturday, and 5.30pm–8.30pm on Tuesday, Thursday and Friday only.

Monasteries and churches

Most monasteries close in the afternoon for two or three hours, though the heavily visited ones remain open all day. If churches are locked, it is polite to respect the privacy of the keyholder during the siesta hours of 1–5pm.

Banks

Typical hours are 8am–2pm, Monday–Thursday and 8am–1.30pm on Friday, but those in major resorts will open until later in the day.

Post offices

Typical hours are 7.30am–2pm Monday–Friday.

Pharmacies

In Greek towns, the ΦΑΡΜΑΚΕΙΟΝ (*Farmakeion*) serves the role of doctor and dispensary – the trained pharmacists who staff them can diagnose most common complaints and recommend a remedy. Though they observe the same opening hours as local shops, there will always be one open on a late-night rota, details of which are posted on pharmacy doors or windows.

Places of worship

Orthodox churches are a prominent feature of every town and village – with luck you will be able to witness a wedding, or a naming ceremony (similar to christening); these usually take place on a Saturday and Sunday, respectively. There are no Protestant, Jewish or Islamic places of worship on Crete, but there are Roman Catholic churches in Iraklíon (on Odós Patros Antoniou) and in Chaniá (just south of the Archaeological Museum).

Police

Crete's tourist police are specifically trained to deal with common visitor problems and most speak English fluently. Many of the complaints they handle (such as cases of overcharging in restaurants and hotels) involve misunderstandings, rather than deliberate fraud, so they are principally there as diplomats to smooth ruffled feathers, but they will also swing into a sympathetic action if you are lost, stranded or just plain confused.

Dial 171 from anywhere and ask for information and help, or you can go to a specific tourist police station.

The main ones are located in the following places:

Iraklíon *on Odós Dhikeosínis 10.*
Chaniá *on Odós Karaiskáki.*
Réthymno *on Prokimeá Venizélou* (i.e. on the beachside road) in the same building as the tourist information office.

Regular police are more unpredictable. Much of the time, they ignore activities that are strictly against the law (parking in prohibited areas, nude or topless bathing, camping rough, breaking the speed limit). Occasionally, however, someone orders a clampdown, so be wary and avoid drawing attention to yourself by behaving in a conspicuous or insensitive manner. Be polite if you are approached by a policeman and usually you will be let off with a warning.

Post

You can buy stamps from kiosks and shops, but they make a small surcharge which you can avoid by going to a yellow post office caravan – these are to be found on the main square of major towns and are open 7.30am–2pm (until 8pm in tourist areas) daily, with reduced hours on Sunday. In Iraklíon, the caravan is on the western side of Plateía Venizélou, by the entrance to the El Greco Park. In Chaniá, it is on the cathedral square, off Odós Hálidhon.

Public transport
Buses

Crete has a comprehensive bus network with hourly services on the busy routes between the four provincial capitals, and four or five services a day on routes covering other parts of the island. Timetables are available at the tourist information offices and at the bus stations in the four main cities. Tickets are purchased in advance from kiosks at the bus terminus, but are sold on board the bus if you join at a stop en route. Prices are low, and the buses are clean and comfortable.

Coaches

Signing up for one of the ubiquitous coach excursions offered by travel agents in every Cretan town is another way of getting to the most popular destinations – the main advantage being that the logistics are all handled for you.

Taxis

Taxis are used for long-distance journeys, as well as short trips across town. There are fixed fares for some journeys but you should always check and agree to the fare in advance to avoid misunderstanding.

Senior citizens

Most museums and archaeological sites have reduced rates for senior citizens. There are few other concessions but, not being tied to school holidays, senior citizens can visit Crete at the quietest and cheapest times of the year. Room rates are lowest in April, May and October and, if you choose to overwinter in Crete, self-catering accommodation is remarkably cheap.

Student and youth travel

Holders of international student identity cards qualify for reduced-price admission to most museums. Crete is, in many respects, a cheap destination, and popular with young people as a result. Some come to Crete for the whole season, doing casual work in bars, tavernas or shops. The pay is poor, or non-existent, but you may be given free accommodation, paid a commission or allowed to keep any tips you might earn.

Sustainable tourism

Thomas Cook is a strong advocate of ethical and fairly traded tourism and believes that the travel experience should be as good for the places visited as it is for the people who visit them. That's why we firmly support The Travel Foundation, a charity that develops solutions to help improve and protect holiday destinations, their environment, traditions and culture. To find out what you can do to make a positive difference to the places you travel to and the people who live there, please visit *www.thetravelfoundation.org.uk*

Telephones

Card-operated pay-phones can be found all over Crete. Coin-operated pay-phones, however, are less common these days.

For long-distance calls, it is cheapest to use a booth accepting phonecards, available from kiosks or shops, or to go to one of the OTE offices (telephone offices) that are found in nearly every town. Calls are metered.

For calls outside Greece, dial *00* + the country code + area code (minus the initial 0) + subscriber number:

Australia *61*   **UK** *44*
Eire *353*   **USA** and **Canada** *1*
New Zealand *64*

For reverse charges, dial the international operator on *161*. You may find it difficult to place an international call at peak times.

Time

Crete is two hours ahead of GMT all year round.

Tipping

Tips are expected on Crete, so round up the figures to the nearest whole number or leave the small change in cafés and tavernas. Taxi drivers expect around 10 per cent, and a small tip should be placed in the toilet attendant's dish before using public facilities. It is also customary to tip tour guides, and priests if they open up the church for you and give you a tour.

Toilets

Public toilets are available in most towns, but often hidden somewhere easy to overlook, so most people use café toilets (which are much better) – having first ordered a drink. Toilet and shower blocks are found at most of the popular beaches, but their cleanliness

varies. Remember, too, that toilet tissues should be put into the wastepaper basket provided.

Tourist information

Branches of the official Greek National Tourist Organisation (GNTO) can be found in the provincial capitals:
Iraklíon *Papa Aleksandrou*
Tel: (2810) 246106/246106.
Nikos Kazantzakis Airport, Iraklíon Arrivals Area
Tel: (2810) 397305/397305.
Chaniá *Kriari 40, Megaro Pantheon*
Tel: (28210) 92943/92943.
Réthymno *Sofokli Venizelou, Megaro Delfini*
Tel: (28310) 29148/29148.
Some useful websites include:
www.creteisland.gr
www.interkriti.org
www.infocrete.com
www.cretetravel.com

Overseas offices of the Greek National Tourist Office are in:
UK *4 Conduit Street, London W1R ODJ. Tel: (020) 7495 9300.*

Travellers with disabilities

Tour operators will tell you which of their villas or hotels is best equipped for travellers who have special needs. A number of the major sights can be visited by booking on to excursions (Knossós included), but the steps and rocky terrain of many of the archaeological sites render them inaccessible to wheelchairs.

Index

Acknowledgements

Thomas Cook Publishing wishes to thank the photographers, picture libraries and other organisations, to whom the copyright belongs, for the photographs in this book.

BIGSTOCKPHOTO 153
DREAMSTIME.COM 1 (FER737NG), 129 (ANNA GURYEVA), 151 (JAVAMAN), 175 (SLAVA296)
CAROLE FRENCH 72, 80, 94, 107, 110, 119, 151, 175
GETTY IMAGES 105
MARY EVANS PICTURE LIBRARY 84, 85
NATURE PHOTOGRAPHERS 149
NEIL SETCHFIELD 31, 32, 55, 58
PHOTOSHOT 93, 109
PICTURES COLOUR LIBRARY 70, 138
THOMAS COOK 96, 148, 163
WORLD PICTURES 30, 53, 82, 92, 114, 115, 136, 154, 157

The remaining pictures are held in the AA PHOTO LIBRARY and were taken by KEN PATERSON, with the exception of pages 13, 16, 18, 19, 22, 23, 28, 44, 45, 46, 47, 49, 52, 65, 75, 78, 101, 106, 108, 109, 111, 131, 133, 161, 182, which were taken by PHILIP ENTICKNAP, and pages 68, 167, taken by WYN VOYSEY.

For CAMBRIDGE PUBLISHING MANAGEMENT LIMITED:
Project editor: Kate Taylor
Typesetter: Paul Queripel
Proofreaders: Jan McCann & Caroline Hunt
Indexer: Marie Lorimer

SEND YOUR THOUGHTS TO BOOKS@THOMASCOOK.COM

We're committed to providing the very best up-to-date information in our travel guides and constantly strive to make them as useful as they can be. You can help us to improve future editions by letting us have your feedback. If you've made a wonderful discovery on your travels that we don't already feature, if you'd like to inform us about recent changes to anything that we do include, or if you simply want to let us know your thoughts about this guidebook and how we can make it even better – we'd love to hear from you.

Send us ideas, discoveries and recommendations today and then look out for your valuable input in the next edition of this title.

Emails to the above address, or letters to the traveller guides Series Editor, Thomas Cook Publishing, PO Box 227, Coningsby Road, Peterborough PE3 8SB, UK.

Please don't forget to let us know which title your feedback refers to!